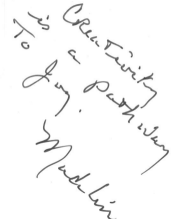

ILLUMINATIONS
The Healing Image

ILLUMINATIONS

The Healing Image

Madeline McMurray

Wingbow Press
Berkeley, California

Wingbow Press books are published and distributed by Bookpeople, 2929 Fifth Street, Berkeley, California 94710.

Library of Congress Cataloging-in-Publication Data

McMurray, Madeline, 1942-
    Illuminations: the healing image / Madeline McMurray. —1st ed. p. cm.
    Bibliography: p.
    ISBN 0-914728-63-6
    1. Art therapy. I. Title.
RC489.A7M35 1988
616.89'1656—dc19

ISBN 0-914728-63-6

Book design by Paula Morrison, Emeryville, California.
Typeset by Campaigne and Somit, Berkeley, California.
Printed by Walsworth Press Company, Inc., Marceline, Missouri.

Front cover: Marc Chagall, *I and the Village*. Collection, The Museum of Modern Art, New York. Oil on canvas, 6′ 3 5/8″ by 59 5/8″. Mrs. Simon Guggenheim Fund. Photograph © 1988 The Museum of Modern Art, New York.

Acknowledgements

The creation of this book has come about through the labors of many souls. Some have contributed directly to the content, while others have been helpers, teachers and supporters. There are too many people to name separately, but each knows who she/he is and we celebrate together this particular illumination. I want to thank David McMurray, for being my best friend through everything; Matina Kilkenny, for the many hours of helping me sort my words; and Dick Brown, for his continual willingness to photograph the images for this book. To Stanton Nelson at Wingbow Press, for transforming my original manuscript into a completed book; to Luella Sibbald for her therapeutic guidance along my journey; to Charlie DiCostanzo for all his work on the original slide show; and to Steve Catton for helping with pictures.

I appreciate and want to thank the numerous friends who have read this text in its early stages as well as all those persons who have agreed to share their personal material in the body of this book. I also want to acknowledge each of my clients for their individual work with the deeply authentic material of their own psyche. It is these people, within this process, who are a continual inspiration to me.

I dedicate this book to Myriam Dardenne. As friend and guide she is a model of commitment and enduring love.

Grateful acknowledgement is made to the following for permission to reprint previously published material:

From *The Secret of the Golden Flower*, by Richard Wilhelm. Copyright 1931. Reprinted by permission of Harcourt Brace Jovanovich, and Routledge and Kegan Paul.

From *Drawing on the Artist Within*, by Betty Edwards. Copyright 1986. Reprinted by permission of Simon & Schuster, Inc.

From *Jung and Tarot: An Archetypal Journey*, by Sallie Nichols. Copyright 1980. Reprinted by permission of Samuel Weiser, Inc., York Beach ME 03910.

From *Drawing on the Right Side of the Brain*, by Betty Edwards. Copyright 1979. Reprinted by permission of Jeremy P. Tarcher, Inc.

From a master's thesis, "Discovering My Personal Myth Through Spontaneous Art Media" by Alice Lloyd Heaton Allen. Sonoma State College, Rohnert Park, California, 1971.

From *Many Winters*, by Nancy Wood. Copyright 1974. Reprinted by permission of Doubleday and Company, Inc.

From *Letters to a Young Poet*, by Rainer Maria Rilke, translated by Stephen Mitchell. Copyright 1984. Reprinted by permission of Random House, Inc.

From *The Myth of Meaning*, by Aniela Jaffe. Copyright 1971. Reprinted by permission of the C.G. Jung Foundation for Analytical Psychology, Inc.

From *Insearch: Psychology and Religion*, by James Hillman. Copyright 1967. Reprinted by permission of Spring Publications.

From *The Awakened Eye*, by Frederick Franck. Copyright 1979. Reprinted by permission of Alfred A. Knopf, Inc.

From *Zen Mind, Beginnner's Mind*, by Shunryu Suzuki. Copyright 1970. Reprinted by permission of John Weatherhill, Inc., of New York and Tokyo.

From *Tao Te Ching*, by Lao Tsu, translated by Gia-Fu Feng and Jane English. Copyright 1972. Reprinted by permission of Random House, Inc.

From *Memories, Dreams and Reflections*, by C.G. Jung, edited by Aniela Jaffe and translated by Richard and Clara Winston. Copyright 1965. Reprinted by permission of Random House, Inc.

From *Lightning East to West*, by James W. Douglass. Copyright 1983. Reprinted by permission of The Crossroad Publishing Company.

From *No Boundary*, by Ken Wilber. Copyright 1979. Reprinted by permission of Shambhala Publications, 314 Dartmouth Street, Boston MA 02116.

From *The Collected Works of C.G. Jung*, translated by R.F.C. Hull, Bollingen Series XX, Volume 8: *The Structure and Dynamics of the Psyche*. Copyright 1960, 1969 by Princeton University Press. Reprinted by permission of Princeton University Press.

William Blake, *The Deity, From Whom Proceed the Nine Spheres*. Courtesy of Ashmolean Museum, Oxford.

Pablo Picasso, *Portrait of Igor Stravinsky*. Paris, May 21, 1920 (dated). Privately owned.

Paul Gauguin, *Head of a Breton Peasant Girl* (c. 1889). Graphite, black and red crayon, black wash on white paper, 224 by 344 mm. Fogg Art Museum, Cambridge, Massachussetts. Bequest - Meta and Paul J. Sachs.

Vincent Van Gogh, *Grove of Cypresses* (1889). Reed pen and ink over pencil on paper, 62.5 by 46.4 cm. Courtesy of The Art Institute of Chicago. Collection: Gift of Robert Allerton.

Marc Chagall, *Pregnant Woman*. Collection Stedelijk Museum, Amsterdam, on loan from Rijksdienst Beeldende Kunst. © ARS, N.Y./ADAGP, 1988.

Table of Contents

The mind never thinks without a mental picture.

—Aristotle

Introduction: Diving for Treasure

In my personal growth and in my professional work as a psychotherapist, I have experienced artistic expression as a doorway to insight, depth communication and healing. A young woman I know once told me, "I go to great lengths to keep my head from exploding." From this, I learned something of what she was going through. But when she provided me with this picture of how she felt, I connected with her in a deeper, more encompassing way. I too have felt what the face in her drawing expressed. Her words filled my mind—her image resounds in my heart.

I recognize that I am primarily a visual learner, but I am not alone. I see the impact of images on my clients' psychological discoveries. When we have ideas that haven't yet touched the depths of the psyche and brought about change, an image can often help us discover the next step. As a painter, I spend time observing life from a visual perspective: form, color, mood and intensity. I've always been sensitive to the impact of images, but only when I began work toward my master's degree in psychology did I become fascinated with the

Explosion

effect of image-making on the psyche.*

Images show us the unknown faces of our own souls and generate the energy needed for change. As a client told me several weeks after creating a particular image, "I don't even know if the image was completely accurate, but from that moment on, my anxiety began to lift and I have felt more relaxed and able to cope." For years I have been creating my own images and watching others do the same. Time and again I have seen image-making open pathways to health.

Ego and Image

A simplified model of the structure of personality separates the known or conscious from the unknown, unconscious aspects of personality, with the ego as the filter between the two. The unconscious consists of layers that are personal, transpersonal, archetypal and collective.

The ego, or who I think I am, controls and shapes these unconscious contents as they move toward consciousness. The role of the ego is to filter the flow of energy from the deeper layers of the psyche and keep the unconscious from flooding us. But by the time most of us are adults what was meant to be fluid has become rigid and limited. Rather than facilitating an exchange between the conscious and the unconscious, the ego most often dominates the unconscious and defines "who I am," restricting the unknown aspects of who I might be or want to become. If my self-image is "I am nice," I do not

---

*The words psyche and soul are used interchangeably throughout this text.

allow the negative dimensions of my unconscious to become known; if I see myself as a loser, I allow no positive qualities into my consciousness.

Through aware and concerted effort, however, the rigid ego can be transformed into an effective participant in the exchange between the two major dimensions of personality.

This book proposes image-making and the development of one's inner artist as a powerful tool for restructuring the ego. The inner artist reaches down into the unconscious and embraces what is available there. She then creates images of her discoveries and presents them to consciousness; the ego can use the images by asking them questions, engaging them in dialogue, learning their meaning, and creating strategies for incorporating these newly-found energies into conscious life.

Image-making is not a difficult undertaking, restricted to those who define themselves as "artistic". It is simply allowing the inner knowledge of who we are and how we feel to appear before us in self-expression through art materials. Throughout this text there are exercises and examples designed to stimulate your image-making capacities. Experiment with image-making by going through the following two exercises step-by-step.

Feelings

The purpose of this exercise is to become more aware of our feelings and our inner life. We respond to all that happens to us, but we seldom take time to consciously hold and examine our reactions.

Begin by selecting the art materials you'd like to use for the exercise. Look over the list in the Appendix (see page 83). After you choose your materials and read through the exercise, allow yourself at least twenty minutes in a quiet location to work on your image-making.

1. Out of your memory pick a particularly strong feeling response that you have had. It could be the result of a recent experience, or one in your past. Early life events often result in strongly-held emotions, positive or negative. The only requirement is that it be intense, because strong feelings teach us the most about ourselves.

2. Sit for five minutes, letting your mind focus on what happened and how you were feeling at the moment. Don't censor what comes and stay with whatever you feel.

3. Rapidly use your chosen materials to create an image of this feeling. What color is it? What motion of hand best expresses it? If the feeling grows stronger, use more than one sheet of paper. Work rapidly and completely. Don't stop until you know that you've depicted the feeling you were focusing on.

4. When the image is complete, write down any words that occurred to you while you were working.

5. Sit looking into your image and reflect on what you see. What does it tell you? Make notes on another piece of paper as ideas come to your mind.

6. Take a few moments to write a clear statement of what you can learn about yourself from this image.

Note: This is an excellent exercise for acknowledging and accepting anger, negative moods and other emotions that we often hold inside because we think that others won't accept us if we express what we feel.

In the next picture, the image-maker began by expressing feelings of depression and inadequacy (the outer ring of the picture). Then he realized that inside his depression was anger. As he expressed this deeper feeling he found the energy to break through his depression.

Feeling Image

Paying Attention

Materials: Again, choose materials that you are comfortable with.

The purpose of this exercise is to bring more attention to your outer life. In any given day we take in an enormous amount of information through our senses, but we often forget the direct effects of events upon us. Most of us frequently allow our minds to lose touch with our surroundings, and we miss both the confusion and the wonder of life. Do you pay attention to what is going on around you or does your mind continually dwell on issues removed from your environment?

1. Begin by going for a walk in a place that you enjoy: a park, an interesting street, a beach, a beautiful part of the city. Be more aware than usual of what goes on around you. What are the sights, the sounds, the smells? Keep your mind free of thoughts that take you away from where you are.

2. Return home and sit quietly. Close your eyes and see what comes to your mind from the walk. What do you remember? People? Things? Colors?

3. Quickly make an image of what you remember: something you saw, a feeling, or simply an expressive color. Don't worry about making a picture of a place, but create a sense of how you experienced your walk.

4. Enjoy what you have created, and let it remind you of your connection to your surroundings and the need to stay awake as you move through life. Environment can nurture and stimulate us when we are attentive to it.

A friend painted this watercolor to recreate a sense of how refreshed she had felt during a walk in the rain. Now, whenever she feels stressed and needs to relax, she can focus again on the image and be nourished by it.

In my work with image-making I have found that Dr. Betty Edwards' books, *Drawing on the Right Side of*

Walking in the Rain

the Brain and *Drawing on the Artist Within*, help me clarify my experiences and observations. Dr. Edwards asserts that "drawings—marks on paper with *or without* recognizable images—can be read like a language and . . . they reveal to the person making the marks (as well as to the viewer) what has been going on in the mind of the mark maker."[1] When I am working with clients on a problem, I often ask them to express the problem itself or their feelings about it, using pen, pencil, or color on paper. The outcome may be random marks or an image. No matter how the visual language presents itself, the image-maker can reflect on and work with the resulting image. I see these illuminations as the aspect of the arts that enables action towards healthier living.

Although Dr. Edwards' work is primarily related to teaching art and mine to psychological growth, our two worlds coincide at the place of seeing. To reach a deeper understanding of this overlap of art and psychology, take the time to experience the following exercise developed by Dr. Edwards.

Drawing a Problem in Analog Form

Please read all of the directions for this exercise before you start your drawing. . . .

1. Scan in your mind's eye various aspects of your current situation, and select one that seems to be causing a problem: something that doesn't fit, or that you don't quite understand. The situation can be a personal one, involving only you, or a situation concerning someone else, or a group of persons, in relation to you. The problem can be related to your career or business, or to a social situation that is of concern to you. It should be a problem, however, whose solution would be a benefit to you and to others in some significant way—in fact, the more important the problem is to you, the better. You will be doing an analog drawing of the selected problem.

2. Do not *name* the problem before you draw. The time will be right to name the problem *after* you have drawn: our aim is to "fly by" the net of words in order to see, and premature naming of the problem may draw in the net of words too closely, perhaps excluding something that is part of the problem. If you say something in words, try to limit the words to "What I know about the situation is . . ." or "What's bothering me is . . ." or "At this point, the way I see it is . . ."

3. . . .(You) *need not* know beforehand what the drawing will look like. Again, the purpose of the drawing is to *find out*. Understand also that you will not solve the problem with this drawing—that is not its purpose. The purpose is to see the situation in a new light, to put it into a new perspective, to "see the picture."

4. Use a pencil for the drawing, and keep an eraser handy.

5. Draw a boundary line as the first step. This is to provide a *format* for the problem—to draw a line around it. The format can be any size or shape you wish, and can be roughly drawn, carefully hand-drawn, or carefully measured and drawn with a straightedge or ruler. This boundary will serve to separate the problem from its

immeasurable surroundings and will allow it to be apprehended as one thing, one unified whole....

6. Do not censor what you draw. Again, this drawing is private and need not be shown to anyone. Summon courage and let the drawing emerge on the paper. Make sure that you draw no objects, no recognizable symbols whatsoever, no words ... —nothing but marks on the paper, the *evidence* of visual thought.

If one drawing seems not to be enough, or if you want to make changes without erasing large areas of the drawing, take another piece of paper and start again— and another, if necessary—as many as you need. Some individuals like to define the problem progressively.

7. *Begin now to draw....*

Regard this drawing as a message from the visual, perceptual part of your mind.... Your task is to apprehend the message, to *read* it.... You—as the apprehender, the viewer of the message—must pass from point to point of the drawing, perceiving the relationship of part to part within the boundaries of the format. Attempt to see the image as a whole and at the same time to see the parts. You are looking for your own thoughts, which will perhaps appear as unexpected or surprising forms. You may have drawn something you didn't expect you would draw. Yet subconsciously, you know the vocabulary of the visual language—its lines, forms, and structures. You know how to read them, and what the drawing *tells*. You know all this because ... you know it. You can see it....

Search your drawing now for new information.[2]

The next image is an example of drawing a problem in analog form. It revealed to its creator that fear prevented his solving a particular problem; he knew what he needed to do but was afraid to do it. Drawing the block led to solving the problem because he saw his fear and worked with it. Energy is wasted on problem-solving if we don't take the time to look at the emotions that surround the problem.

The inner artist can express feelings, reflect situations and draw problems in analog form. She knows the complete self well enough to uncover conflicts and reach the dimension of the unconscious that holds the possibility of healing.

Fear

Many of us can't find the inner artist because we fear self-expression and facing the undeveloped parts of ourselves. Our fear feeds neurotic and negative attitudes and neglects the healing aspect within us. Our feelings surface to awareness during times of self-examination; then our fear of expression lessens and we are open to new discoveries.

Looking inward empowers us to create images that teach us about our unknown dimensions. Image-making expresses what seemed inexpressible. We can depict anxiety, fear, delight and sorrow. They come alive in color and form, to be examined and understood. We can be more objective and perceive ourselves more clearly. By witnessing our behaviors we reduce the power contained in various emotional states; we can look pain, struggle, hidden desires and old wounds in the face, name them, ask them questions, give them their own voices through the language of images, and grant these diverse and shadowy elements a role in transformation and growth.

The inner artist can go beyond issues of personal transformation to the collective dimensions of the unconscious, revealing images of our shared situation and giving us the opportunity to question and converse with them. We are, after all, more than individual; we share in the cultural-historical development of humankind. When I work with groups on questions of planetary survival in the nuclear age, I apply the belief of Robert Lifton that we must learn to deal with "end-of-the-world imagery" if we are to respond creatively to our world situation.[3]

A woman reflecting upon end-of-the-world imagery created this teardrop image. She wrote:

The sun feels so warm on my face
The breeze flows through my hair
The green leaves smell so good
I hear the gentle birds
and touch the warm hand of my neighbor.
I am alive
and the heavens cry!

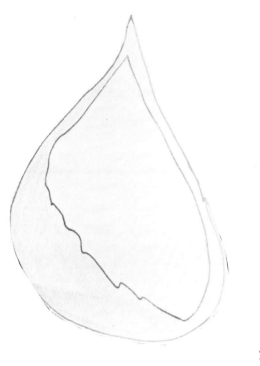

Teardrop

7

Through this experience with image-making she was able to focus not only on her despair for the world, but on her love for it. She asked herself how she could participate in planetary healing and she uncovered what action best suited her personality.

From personal development to planetary concerns, we find solutions to life problems by creating images and responding to our illuminations. Through the creativity of the inner artist, we gain new insight and release psychic energy that was tied up in destructive habits of the ego. Awareness of our own images stimulates us to become more than we presently know. It is as if the gardener can look at the seed and see the plant that has yet to appear and the fruit that it will bear.

This book is designed to enable you to enjoy the fruits of your own inner artist—to experience the creative healing resources within the world of the individual psyche. The danger in reading about images is that the language of the intellect may distance you from the life-giving energy of creating images. In hopes of counterbalancing the written word, this book presents many images from my own work as well as those of clients, friends and renowned artists. The images and exercises throughout the book are meant to encourage you to participate in self-discovery through image-making. People did not merely think about these images; they manifested them.

Image-making, putting the image into concrete form rather than allowing it to float loose in the mind, eventually to be lost, is step one. Once created, each image was reflected on, written about, or in some way used to increase the image-maker's self-awareness. This is step two: image-using. These two practices, image-making and image-using, are the core of this book. As we go through the processes described here, we come to know the living experience of freeing creative energy for psychological and spiritual growth.

1

Art as Healer

Personal Perspective

My interest in art began when I was a college student, but I didn't do much with it until years later, after my two oldest children were born. Upon becoming a full-time mother I found that I yearned for something totally my own and separate from the family. I had a woman friend who also had two small children and this same yearning. We supported one another in this need to be something more than "mothers". Once a week we hired childcare and spent the day doing art together. I realize now that we were providing ourselves with the best possible therapy. A day of creativity, away from the demands of preschool children, would restore anyone's sense of well-being. We simply saw ourselves as a bit "indulgent" and never gave much thought to things like psychotherapy.

I gradually became more involved in my art work, taking classes in painting and drawing. I primarily painted lively impressionistic landscapes. The contrast between suburban-city life (which appeared to me flat,

gray and chaotic) and country life (which I saw as dynamic, vibrant and peaceful) created a conflict that I eventually resolved by moving from the suburbs to the country. At the same stage in my life I learned meditation practices. Through these two activities, art and meditation, my perception of life changed dramatically.

After five years of country living, I became interested in the theories of Carl Jung. My chosen isolation was six hours' drive from the nearest Jungian analyst, so I arranged to see a therapist once a month with multiple sessions each trip. I thus began a process of long-distance psychotherapy and was challenged to find a way to deal with the events of my psyche between sessions. The logical approach was to paint or draw my psychological unfolding, but it was very difficult for me to paint what I felt at that time because I had begun to uncover so much anger and negativity.

My own ways of thinking, as well as my artistic definitions and standards, blocked my freedom of expression. I didn't believe that painting nightmares was art and I was caught up in trying to portray what I thought rather than what I felt. Eventually, I decided to paint only from my personal world without correction or judgment. I had to let go of technique and allow what wanted to be expressed to come onto the paper. Free of the outer artist, I began to experience the impact of image-making at the hands of the inner artist.

Very early in analysis I was confronted with a terrifying dream in which I was with a dark woman in a car at night. This woman was driving too fast and becoming more and more reckless so I yelled at her to slow down. At that moment she looked at me and I saw that she was a witch, quite content with what was happening. I was sure she would kill us both. I startled myself awake and lay in my bedroom in the dark, my heart pounding. I was afraid to turn on the light because I still felt this witch's presence.

At last, when I reached for the light and found my room free of such a being, I said "It was only a dream." Nonetheless, I was still filled with fear and could not return to sleep. I sat up in bed and began to draw my fearful feelings. What appeared on the paper was the face of my dream. I was turning the page of my journal to begin a second image when I caught the outline of the woman's head on the back page. As the light shown through her hair I saw that although she was a witch, she had other aspects to her character that I hadn't seen before. My fears were quieted now and I began to write a dialogue with this figure from my dream.

Dark one, why are you so fearful to me?
Because you ignore me. I need your attention. I need to matter.

The Witch Woman

What can I do?
Affirm me.
I don't understand.
It is dark down here, I need light. Bring me into the day that I might live.
What is your name?
Undiscovered Life.

In a few short moments in the middle of the night my witch woman was transformed into possible new life. I could now turn off the light and go back to sleep. Later this image was re-examined in a therapy session and I became more familiar with this darker side, or shadow, of my personality. The shadow is the part of each of us that is rejected, hidden and projected outward to be seen in other people.[4] It is power-filled and, in the image of the dream cited above, can drive us out of control and endanger our well-being. But embracing one's shadow and coming to know it more fully bring new energy for daily living.

I was confronted with an aspect of myself that I didn't like, didn't want to know, refused to be responsible for, and criticized readily in others. Changes in my relationship to my shadow helped me name my own darkness: for example, my negative intensity and pushiness. As I learned to accept my own intensity—my witch—I could feel less negative about myself, as well as other intense and pushy people. By remembering that my witch also represented possibilities of life, I could more easily accept her and work for her inclusion as part of my self-image.

We can't deal with aspects of our personality that we've rejected, and we can't change what we refuse to look at. What we learned as children is part of our psyche. We learned to reject aspects of ourselves, not necessarily because they were innately bad, but because our parents, teachers and peers rejected them. The struggle with the shadow now causes us to be both rejected and rejecter. It takes time and patience to incor-porate these rejected parts back into ourselves and live comfortably with who we really are, rather than who we were taught to be or would like to be.

As the unacceptable becomes acceptable, negative responses weaken; what would earlier have been a difficulty or even a disabling neurosis often ceases to be an issue at all. For example, my anger at a woman professor who was always late for class dissipated as I understood that like her, I was stretched too thin and wasn't handling the details of my life any better than she was.

Acknowledging our shadow leads to compassion and understanding both for ourselves and others. Our personal conflicts as well as planetary power struggles reveal the uncontrolled shadow and our collective lack of humility and compassion. We see our darkness in the world around us and self-righteously blame others: Our condition and that of the world are someone else's fault. Recognizing our shadow as a constant companion is part of the path to humility—a quality needed in our personal and collective lives.

As I became more familiar with these rejected parts of myself, I felt more sensitive, not only to myself but to life in general. Raindrops, flowers, bird songs—all seemed so delicate, and I found myself completely involved in making images of plant life. I could imagine how the natural cycles of life, death and rebirth applied to me. Winter trees filled my mind and I often sat drawing them, wondering about their essence. I drew a series of nature images that spoke to me of growth as both natural and mysterious at the same time. I titled these images *New Growth* and let nature teach me what I

New Growth

environment, has been a difficult struggle for me. My desire to establish order and make things happen has given way to an attitude of letting things happen and a willingness to participate in life as it evolves.

Regulating my lifestyle and quieting my attempts to do everything at once have been necessary for the development of these more positive dimensions of myself. The value of my "new growth" stance is that I can now embrace my life situation from a broader perspective. As Nancy Wood says, "Nature does not fight against anything."[5]

Released from the grip of the shadow side, I experienced the first delicate expressions of healing in the integration of the multiple aspects of my life. While I became more acquainted with personal growth as a natural unfolding, I realized that, like many plants, I required tending. I examined what in my psyche was threatening the development of my new possibilities. I constantly experienced the new parts of my soul's development being smothered, as though there were too many weeds in my garden for the sapling of patience and understanding to have the space and light it needed to flourish. I felt frustrated at not being in touch with what I knew to be a healing process. I felt a more balanced attitude about my life, but maintaining this balance was difficult; I was overwhelmed by the belief that I must do more: "Be a better wife, a better mother, a better student, and certainly be more serious about my psychological growth and development." Whose words were these?

I felt split apart by this driving voice in my mind and I considered myself inadequate when unable to do

would need to withstand if I were to bloom perennially.

There was a hard lesson in this process that I was only beginning to grasp. Growth, by nature's standards, includes birth, seasons and death, while growth by my mind's definition simply meant taking action. Learning to accept natural growth, subject to the influence of my everything. I was caught in negative judgments rather than starting from an attitude of self-acceptance and affirmation. These two ways of functioning—one out of balance and discordant, the other balanced and harmonic—were opposing pulls in my personality, and for most of a year I vacillated between them. I needed to take the next step to reach solid ground and stop wavering.

At last a dream enabled me to move out of this pull of opposing forces. Although it was frightening, I had become more accustomed to accepting dark images, so my fear was not as great as in my earlier work. In this dream I saw a huge bird sweeping across the face of the moon. For many days the image returned to my mind's eye and caused me to wonder. I realized that I must paint what I was seeing.

When the painting was complete I still didn't understand what it meant. I placed it in a corner of my room and each day I reflected a little on its possible meaning. I began to realize that this was more than my shadow; it was something deeper in me that could devour what I knew was natural, healing and feminine. I worked alone and with my analysts on this image and others like it in a very intense three-month period. The word that always came up in connection with these images was *Devourer*.

Because they touched painful events in my childhood, I had to accept that they revealed a wound that would not be healed easily or soon. I could either encourage "new growth" and healing to overcome the negative impact of this particular self-discovery, or let the wound continue to devour me. With the help of the inner artist I

Devourer

could keep the images in my awareness. Each day I took a few minutes to color my moods (see "Working With Color," page 34) and check in with myself as to how much I was affected by this personal darkness. The inner artist, much to my surprise, often came up with more growth images to remind me that darkness was also part of my life, that my intensity of feeling was all right and that I would eventually see a more complete picture. I was re-experiencing the loss of my primary male figures (the deaths of my father and grandfather); I needed time for healing.

Negative judgments still flowed freely from the "Devourer," but now I could look more clearly at my situation and determine how things were going. If my professors gave me good grades for my work, why give authority to the inner voice that said "I'm doing a lousy job"? If my children were getting along fine with their peers and teachers, why believe a voice that told me, "I'm not an adequate mother"? I learned that I didn't have to accept those negative judgments, and I began to feel the freedom of living a satisfying and fulfilling life.

The power of the negative voice inside me was diminishing, but I still felt some block to my own life potential. The out-of-balance pull took on a different aspect, and I began to identify it as the negative animus.* I found this negative part of my personality stronger than any of my previously experienced inner figures. It was connected only to the "rational" aspects of my mind and dismissed my emotional needs. It could justify any-

thing, including my leaving family and friends to take care of themselves while I pursued my own development. Never did it admit that this development would only be partial unless I related to those around me, or that separation would have harmful emotional consequences. I was moving away from my family and taking on new professional roles where I needed more focused energy, but not all the aggression that resulted. As I worked with this negative side, I began to ask myself if there was anything positive to be salvaged from it.

I was both drawn to and repelled by this intellectual, aggressive, competitive part of myself. It held a great deal of seductive power. It said I could judge and reject anyone or anything while demanding separation from responsibilities and commitments. If a colleague, friend or family member asked me to do something that I didn't want to do, I could now refuse, invoking the importance of *my* work, *my* time, *my* way. Where once I had been too easygoing about my roles and relationships, I was now sharp-edged and unwilling to give to those who weren't connected to what I was pursuing. The emotional cost to me was the loss of some old friendships, and the start of new relationships that later proved fruitless.

For some time I struggled to understand how this dark figure in my psyche could be woven into my personality. A wrestling match was taking place inside me. Dark and murderous dreams pursued me, and my only escape from them was to wake up. The impact of an alcoholic father who died an early death, a dominant mother and a passive but harsh stepfather had combined

---

*This term and its definition "masculine side of a woman's personality" represent the classic Jungian approach to these aspects of a woman's personality. Although these were helpful constructs at the time of my analysis, today I prefer defining these same elements as part of my total feminine psyche as clarified in Jean Shinoda Bolen's *Goddesses in Everywoman*.[6]

in my psyche in a very threatening way. As I learned to identify this dimension of myself and give it a face, the name *Disease* came to mind. I had to work at keeping this diseased one contained so that it would not infect the rest of me. This was a time when new growth was going slowly; I had to keep the negative aspects under control and wait for the next development.

I knew that life events influenced my personality, but to blame my family would be to avoid recognizing the dark elements in my present psyche. It helped to understand their origin, but I still had to do something about their transformation. I found that I needed much strength to withstand this force inside me. It became an even greater challenge to keep some sense of balance. But if I related to my family and friends in a creative way, if I remembered to give myself space for play and freedom from responsibility, and if I allowed time for meditation, rest and relaxation, "disease" was contained and I was no longer fighting myself.

In time "disease" began to change. Images of unease and unrest still came to me but I knew that something about them was beneficial, if a little unnerving. As this new energy arose from old images, I understood that only by facing my negative side could I use its power for positive development. I could put my critical judgment to work choosing what I needed; it would help me decide how to complete my work while keeping the various aspects of my life in harmony. This wrestling match was beginning to turn in my direction, and like Jacob wrestling with the angel, I was receiving a blessing. A dream in which my dead father phoned to ask how

Disease

he could help me validated my search for understanding. I knew that my old wounds were now beginning to heal. This healing set in motion a search for deeper knowledge. The wounds had not been neatly taken away, but now I knew that what had once caused harm could also give life. Like Jacob I might thereafter walk with a limp, but I would not lose my blessing.

Transitional Perspective

The next set of images, which I call the *Wild Beasts*, was more archetypal in nature and appeared in the form of serpents and dragons. The various dimensions of the unconscious present themselves in forms that are both personal, like those shared above, and archetypal. I was entering the more archetypal domain of my psyche. I had always been fearful of this part of myself because it usually appeared in outbursts of anger and was not at all acceptable to other people. I tried to keep this part of my psyche hidden. How to come to terms with the passion and natural forcefulness of my personality was my next challenge.

My first response was to meet these wild beasts with sword in hand and, like St. George, quickly slay them. Fortunately, the artist in me was fascinated with their wildness and since I was trying to release myself from being driven, dogmatic and self-righteous, I let the inner artist have her way. I began to portray these creatures and talk with them in active imagination* as part of image-using.

While creating images of my wild ones I listened to them and asked them questions; when our conversations were finished I made notes of what was said. I quickly discovered that the wild beasts were playful, full of life and guardians of great treasure. Once, as I was exploring what my Spirit Guide might be, a great red dragon presented itself and I realized that these mighty beasts are not for killing.

Nor are they for taming. They are for listening to and learning from. I read stories and myths about dragons and sought out depictions of them in art. Wild creatures do not have to be destructive or harmful. In

The Wild Beasts

---

*Robert Johnson describes active imagination as "a dialogue that you enter into with the different parts of yourself that live in the unconscious. In some ways it is similar to dreaming, except that you are fully awake and conscious during the experience."[7]

China, for example, the dragon is a figure of wisdom and is celebrated. The serpent in the Garden of Eden has too often been interpreted as Satan, the Evil One, and we have missed the creative possibility of this image. In Genesis, "The serpent was the most subtle of all the wild beasts that Yahweh God had made" and it gave us knowledge of good and evil.[8] This may be fearful, but it is not something to be avoided.

At first, staying with the dragons seemed a risky business. I feared their burning breath. Much of what we fear is carried in the psyche by images of the untamed. Magnificent wild horses, power-filled bulls, primitive tribal dancers in ceremonial dress and majestic larger-than-life buffalo are all images that people have shared with me about this part of themselves. It is a connection to deeper layers of the soul. We fear it, not because of its strength, but because of its Otherness. It is complex and confusing so we hold back. The inner artist reveals our relationship to it by working with these great and powerful archetypes, and opens the doorway to wider dimensions of the human personality.

Embracing my wild beasts meant standing in the presence of my own fire and in turn facing the fires of the world. Today I am more willing to deal with the threat of worldwide destruction and work for collective transformation because I'm aware of the creative possibility in these overpowering energies. I can confront such forces as I meet them in myself, in others, and in the world. As I have learned not to run from my tensions or fears, the powers that seemed to threaten me turn out instead to be the bearers of great gifts. To quote Rainer Maria Rilke:

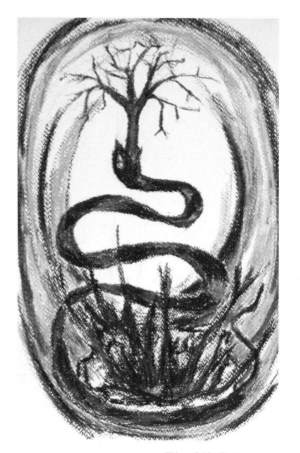

The Gift Bringer

Perhaps all the dragons in our lives are princesses who are only waiting to see us act, just once, with beauty and courage. Perhaps everything that frightens us is, in its deepest essence, something helpless that wants our love.[9]

Guardian of the Center

By depicting the archetypal energy in our psyche, we can name it and learn to value what we have been neglecting. Like Moses, who dared to look upon the burning bush, we are offered vast possibilities. We must not hold back from meeting the dragons of our personal or collective life, for dragons guard the treasure of the soul; if we fail to meet them, the substance of our very being will remain undiscovered.

Many people stop working at growth through image-making just as they reach this transition towards the archetypal unconscious because they are no longer struggling with the personal issues that were the initial reason for their work. At this point of development, they must choose to pursue their relationship to the unconscious or the ego will take on the role of maintaining their new self-image at the expense of future growth.

Once the connection to the unconscious is clearly developed, there is the danger of being fascinated with the archetypal images of the soul and staying with them at the cost of contact with what Jung termed the Self—"the image of God within the human psyche."[10] The work of interweaving the conscious and unconscious in their personal and archetypal imagery is a neverending unfolding.

As I came to know my "Wild Beasts" and how they fit into my life, I began to enter the next stage of archetypal images on my journey towards the Self—the realm of angels.

Knowledge and wisdom are available in many of the images of ourselves from which we turn away. Our task is to stand our ground long enough to listen to them and receive the gift they might offer.

Transpersonal Perspective

We tend to think of angels as little white winged beings hovering over manger scenes, but they are much more diverse. Angels can be as small as dewdrops in the fairy world, or in biblical tradition, stand seven feet tall and carry flaming swords. Sometimes they speak with doves flying from their mouths, and sometimes with lightning bolts. They personify the psychoid factor in that they have a "paradoxical nature which is both material and spiritual."[11] The angel functions in my psyche as the voice of the Self and is always unpredictable by my standards. For me the divine archetypes have most often been angels, while for others they might appear as goddesses, prophets, saints or Zen masters.

A radiant being appears to me in a dream and says quite boldly and simply: "The Buddha is in the same dimension as the Christ." I awaken knowing that I've learned an important lesson: My love of Buddhism and my Christian background are united in my psyche, and the conflicts I've often felt about them can now be released. In meditation, angels present themselves like lightning, flashing biblical quotes or statements from Zen teachings through my mind. The impact of these spoken messages is a clarity of mind that I did not have before. Angel voices override the spinning of my restless thinking.

We're tempted to try to touch the Self without applying the experience to daily life. The whole idea of getting "high" reflects the inability or unwillingness to

The Angel Messenger

live with our wild beasts and angels in ordinary ways. We want to touch the inner world when it feels good, but if it makes demands upon us, we rapidly retreat. The angels, like dragons, make demands—the demands of the

Self—and we wrestle as much with this dimension of the psyche as we do with the dark parts of our personal wounds. It is not true that if we knew what to do, we would do it. Angels come in dreams, visions, crises and turmoil but their messages go unheard and unheeded.

For all the wonder and wisdom of the angels, they have a way of connecting us to reality with very simple challenges. They can yell loudly and rudely, "Are you awake?" and "Do you remember what we teach?"

Once, while feeling very smug about my most recent insight, I was walking across my yard believing enlightenment to be just around the corner. Suddenly I was sharply smacked in the face by one very oversized icy raindrop which broke my great religious moment and threw me into a fit of laughter over my own pomposity. It is the angel in me that can laughingly set me free from my own inflation.

My involvement with angels—reading about them, painting them and writing dialogues with them—brought me to a new and important understanding of the relationship between angels and wild beasts. The complexity of the Self involves holding these archetypal forces together at the center of our being. I received a dream message saying "Never be fooled—wild beast or angel—all are messengers of God." This statement connects to Shunryu Suzuki's lesson of "the oneness of duality": "Not Two, and not one."[12] The unity and complexity of our center are the gateway to greater wholeness—the meeting place of personal and transpersonal. This wholeness is not an end to be attained, but a dynamic exchange and activity; it connects to the whole

The Dance of Wholeness

of one's life, as one's life connects to all life. This picture of reality reflects our connection and interdependence with all life on Planet Earth.

Reflecting on the progression of these images, we can see their overall order unfolding. They begin by dealing with personal issues, lead to the transpersonal, and develop a relationship between the personal and transpersonal dimensions of the psyche: the Ego-Self axis.[13] Growth is a spiral. Personal issues are always a living part of reality; we do not transcend them. Through relationship to the Self we are more than our personal issues. Jesus' teaching to love God with all and love your neighbor as yourself is an excellent illustration of the ego-Self-world connection.

Interestingly enough, we do everything at the same time; we embrace God while discovering the model of how to love our neighbor through loving ourselves. We don't act in only one dimension, i.e., "I'll work on myself and then do something in the world," "I'll walk the spiritual path and everything else will take care of itself," or "When the world is in better condition I can work on myself"—we are challenged to learn to develop an ever-expanding and inclusive perspective.

The Feminine Connection

Affirmations

As I wrestled to incorporate the images and words presented by the work of the inner artist, a bridge was growing between the known and the unknown parts of myself, affirming my work on image-making: an affirmation of all the elements of life in their positive and negative forms. Life still involved struggle, but the struggle took on more significance because I connected it to a sense of the sacred presence within and around me. As part of this affirmation, three dynamic and exciting images presented themselves to me, confirming the progress of my image-making/image-using.

The first was a mature feminine figure struggling to embrace life in its multiple aspects. Her words were: "By coming to know the depths of your own soul you can know something of the complexity and the compassion of the divine." I saw this image as myself, my particular I, connected to the inner and outer dimensions at the same moment, making all one. I also saw this figure as the human potential rising in the world around me: the

The Holy Fool

selves, but the whole.

The second image of affirmation was inspired by Charles Williams' image of the Fool in his book *The Greater Trumps*.[14] The Fool as life dancer wanted to be explored and my inner artist began to create an image. Here the Fool is one who has experienced being healed as well as healing. As James Hillman says: "Healing comes from our unguarded side, from where we are foolish and vulnerable. This is expressed by the idea of the wounded healer, who heals through his own wounds...."[15]

This Fool image is the part of me that dances on the healing path to the Center and back again, accepting all the elements of life. It reveals knowledge of change and reminds me that there is something in each of us that can juggle the orb of the world, dance with dragons and stay open to the movement of the Holy Spirit. This image reminds me of the connection between my small self and my greater Self, between personal and collective, between mine and Ours. The dance of the Fool has enabled me to become a risk-taker. The more I dance and the more the Fool dances in me, the more I see the relationship between my life and all life.

My psychic development, leading to its transpersonal aspect and its connection to the whole of life, is shared with the world; each of us is a manifestation of the same source. We all serve the same purpose on this planet, to be human beings. But we suffer, and our Earth suffers, because of our limited vision. As I evolve with the unfolding of my own images I see that in our suffering lies our potential for personal and planetary healing if we meet and transform the elements of our lives.

element of the psyche that can evoke unity and healing in each of us while restoring health to our wounded world. If each of us is a microcosm of the greater macrocosm, then our healing and our actions affect not only our-

My third image was a Goddess figure who held Sun and Moon while walking with her feet upon the Earth. She spoke of the energy in each human soul that must be enlivened if healing for the world is to come into being. She brought the vision of the citizens of "New Day" and she spoke for the glorious possibility of fullness of life on this splendid planet—Earth.[16]

These last two images, *Holy Fool* and *Citizen of New Day*, are expressions of the sacred function in the human psyche. Each in its own way holds together the opposites of the universe: Sun and Moon, Dragon and Dove, Heaven and Earth. This union of opposite forces creates a new life energy. Again we are reminded, "not Two, and not one." These images speak of what is greatest in the soul of humankind. Through this greatness we can gently work to restore the natural balance of life that has been disrupted in us and in our world.

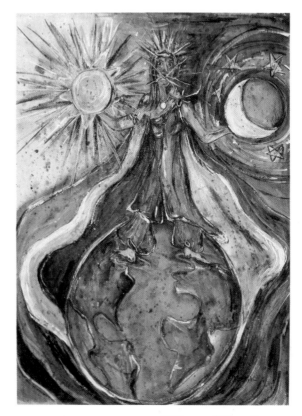

Citizen of New Day

The Spiral Design

2

The Inner Artist

The perspective of the inner artist includes a continuum that runs from the "inventory of self-absorption" to a larger awareness of "unity consciousness."[17,18] It is not unusual to find people stuck at one or the other end of this continuum. One person might come to counseling because job-related stress is manifested in anxiety that makes everyday functioning difficult. When the anxiety is released through exercises or biofeedback, he makes some small adjustment to being anxious, and goes on with his work, accepting this as the way life is.

Another person may come to therapy wanting to do "transpersonal work." After a number of sessions it becomes clear that despite diligent work with larger-scale concepts of purpose and meaning, she does not connect these ideas to the personal and interpersonal levels of her life.

The inner artist can be helpful for both of these people. In the first case there is the opportunity to expand his worldview, and in the second the inner artist can help bring that worldview into daily reality. The inner artist dances along this continuum between self-absorption and unity consciousness. Every life event contains elements of both perspectives, and we are enriched and expanded when we knowingly include both. The following experience, related by the artist Frederick Franck, illustrates this continuum and its restorative quality.

...I was driving to New York from my home in Warwick. I had gone a few miles when I switched on my radio for the news.

"Explosions are heard as far as Tel Aviv ... huge columns of tanks are crossing the Suez Canal ..." it said.

My heart seemed to skip: "Another war!"

Once more a flashback. I was not in school yet ... A mile south of my hometown, across the Belgian border, the First World War had started. Stiff with horror I saw the flaming town of Visé from our attic window. The constant booming of the big guns was to accompany my childhood ... It was the beginning of the barbaric sequence of bloodbaths that has continued ever since.

"I've had it!", I heard myself shout. For a split second I was suicidal, almost drove my car into a tree. Instead I stopped.

On my left a meadow was gently rising toward a blue sky with white clouds, a meadow full of purple and white autumn flowers. Where meadow and sky met stood a fringe of feathery trees. I took my sketchbook, climbed halfway up the slope, sat down and started to draw the grasses, thistles, flowers, the wispy trees.

"Behold, all flesh is as the grass" from Brahms' Requiem came back to me . . . After a while I noticed that my agitation had ebbed away. Not the sadness, nor the despair, but the turmoil and the black anger. I had found a still point, my center.

Still you are here . . . still here: meadow, grass, Queen Anne's lace . . . beloved Earth! I am still here! My eyes still see! I and this meadow, I and these grasses . . . we are NOT-TWO . . . Escape from reality? Oh no!! Escape into Reality! IN THE MIDST OF FOLLY AND TERROR: THE LIFELINE TO THE SOURCE RETRIEVED.[19]

Here we see the artist in a moment of personal conflict choosing to connect to his greater reality. The relationship between person and nature brings healing through image-making, expanding awareness and energy for a fuller life. The inner artist embraces this perspective, the "escape into reality."

The value of contact with nature is also clear to my clients. When I ask what helps them relax and recover a sense of balance in their lives, what restores and refreshes them: Again and again, their answer is nature. Unfortunately, many people, even country dwellers, lead lifestyles that make nature a luxury to be experienced primarily on weekends and vacations.

But while we can't always make the healing journey to nature, one of the delightful gifts of the inner artist is that she enables us to find a balance point to our lives in the space of our own living rooms, as the following exercise will show.

Restoring Balance

When we are out of balance we either feel overwhelmed by personal problems and don't know how to make things better, or we avoid those problems by roaming in the world of ideals without a sense of satisfaction. Either way, life is not as fulfilling as it might be.

Materials: a felt tip pen and a piece of paper

1. Unplug your telephone. Put on a piece of your favorite music, sit comfortably and relax.

2. Close your eyes and listen to the music you've chosen. Put all your problems aside. As you begin to feel relaxed, put the tip of the pen down any place on the paper. Let the pen roam. Listen to the music and let the pen move with it. Don't think about what you are doing.

3. As you watch yourself making lines on the paper, see if an image surprises you. Do you see something in your lines? When you discover something, retrace what you

see and build an image out of what you've started.

4. The image created here may be concrete like the *Open Face* or the *Spiral Design* (see page 24), or it may be abstract like a doodle. Whatever happens, let it come. Don't try to define it—let it create itself through you.

5. When you feel you have done enough, put your art in front of you. Examine it from different perspectives.

6. Write a few sentences about what the inner artist has created. If you feel a deep connection to what has come out, you might want to develop it further through writing or active imagination. If you feel it isn't saying anything, don't push or worry about it. The relaxation and sense of restored balance are what you were seeking. The insight is an added benefit.

Note: This is a good exercise to experiment with in a variety of media. You might want to try finger paints or a ball of clay.

The Open Face

We prevent ourselves from solving problems or coming to terms with the issues of life because we can only see the picture of the world that we already know. Behaviors are often nothing more than habits that we believe in. When we complain about our work or our relationships we describe them through our own limited vision. We see most of life as though it were set in concrete, and we think that we can't change or that "they won't change" while we keep the order around us solidly the same. Our inner artist can bring us perspectives that we have not yet considered. We need only allow her the opportunity.

I once saw a client who was depressed, disappointed in many of the people he knew. As he used image-making to examine these people, he saw that they too were sad and disappointed. This insight allowed him to stop expecting others to meet his needs, for they had their own problems, and to reach out to those around him. Life itself can change as the images of its possibilities change.

Creative expression brings with it the opportunity for a new beginning and must not be left dormant simply because one's self-image does not include having talent. On her first visit to my office a client told me in no uncertain terms that she hated art and would not touch the materials on my desk because her mother was "the artist in the family". This client is now experiencing the value of self-discovery through drawing; she creates art readily in our sessions and is very receptive to what her images have to teach her. Her artist-mother instilled perfectionism about art, as well as many other things, in her at an early age, and the child gave up art because she could not please her mother. Now that she is an adult, she has worked her way out of her self-confining models of perfection and is free to explore her own expressive abilities.

Like this woman, we often consider ourselves "not able" while seeing others as talented, creative and artistic. We leave art to the professionals and go our unfulfilled way. The creative spirit, often stunted in childhood, lies dormant and undeveloped in most of us.

Not all of us had parents who inhibited our ability to express ourselves, but the world around us gives artistic activity the status of daydreaming and wasting time. The child who dares to draw pictures in school other than during art period quickly learns that one's time is better spent on other projects. Education comes from both family and society around us, and as a rule almost everything is given precedence over creative expression. I grew up with a focus on the sciences in school because we Americans had to beat the Russians in the space race.

Unfortunately it wasn't until I was much older that I learned about the great Russian authors and the wonder of the Russian ballet.

Because of this limited education in childhood, we must re-educate ourselves and open doors that have long been closed. We may in fact need a modern-day Renaissance to free ourselves from the present dominance of technology and science. Our present educational system is primarily based upon test scores and a vocabulary that is seldom, if ever, visual. Unfortunately, the less orderly and more spontaneous processes of creativity do not lend themselves to numerical description. Thus, from the earliest years, education encourages rational, linear, logical thinking and discourages the intuitive, irrational nature of personality. Rather than value the indescribable and the unmeasurable, this system leads us to dismiss our own creative resources. If we compare the number of computer classes appearing in our grammar schools to those in storytelling, creative writing, music and art, we can see the dominance of the scientific/technological model.

We are influenced by our childhood attitudes and experiences; we were educated to a particular self-image and worldview that still keep us from discovering our own creative energy. We must confront the barriers in our present attitudes and heal the inner split which tells us that artistic expression comes as some special gift to only a chosen few. We must face the neglect of our inner artist and work to encourage the development of our own creative/healing resources.

3

Overcoming the Critic

When we approach the arts, the first figure we most often meet is our own inner critic. It tries to destroy the inner artist, our self-image and life around us. This critic says "I can't," "That isn't good enough," "This is a waste of time," "I'm not an artist," and anything else it can come up with to repress creativity. This negative voice must be controlled if we are to express our images. The inner artist can gain authority over this critic by portraying its face and asking, "Where does this voice come from, and why is it so powerful?"

I have not yet met the individual who could claim no knowledge of this inner negating voice. The following exercise is designed to bring this voice into conscious awareness so that it might be contained, learned from and transformed.

Facing the Critic

Materials: Have on hand writing paper and pen, a pencil, a box of oil pastels or crayons and drawing paper. Read through all of the instructions before beginning. Allow approximately a half an hour.

1. First, listen to and record your own critical voice as it involves itself in your daily life. The inner critic can be identified by both its unwillingness to let an issue drop and its tendency to flood into many aspects of your life. For example, you may have forgotten to make a bank deposit. Naturally, you reprimand yourself, make the deposit, and go on your way. But if you are still thinking about your "foolish mistake" hours or even days later, you can be sure the critic is at work. If a mistake becomes a theme and you find yourself remembering apparently unrelated personal flaws and errors, it is time to quiet this overactive critical voice.

2. Sit down and take five minutes to write a list of everything this voice says to you.

3. Now read the list back to yourself. Let the critical voice ring inside your mind. As you hear it, let an image begin to form.

4. Draw the image that comes to you, showing what it feels like to hear this critical voice. Trace the image over and over, letting it grow in strength of color and form.

5. There will be a few primary thoughts in your mind; write them down on the same page with the image. A word or two will be adequate.

6. Sit quietly, letting the image and words reflect your own critical processes back to you. As you do this, let a question arise inside your mind and write it down. (The only requirement here is that this question be open-ended, not be answerable with a yes or no.) You could begin by asking "Why are you so negative?" or "Where do you come from?"

7. Spend a few minutes writing the answer you hear in your mind. Do not labor over this; allow yourself to be spontaneous.

8. Consider what you need to do about this critical voice. Make notes as to what you have learned from this exercise.

9. The next time you hear this voice resounding in your head, recall the image that you have made during this exercise and reflect again on what to do about the inner critic.

It is useful to practice this exercise on a regular basis until you know the inner critic's many faces well enough to catch it in action and use its energy in a more positive way.

A client who took the time to draw this face and listen to this voice in herself provides an example of working with the critic. As she drew the face of her critic she nicknamed him "Old Red Eyes." Simply by giving the critic a name, she began to free herself from his authority over her. In working with the image and writing down the discoveries that presented themselves, she learned that it was "Old Red Eyes" who said that she was not good enough. He asked "Why would anybody want anything to do with me?" and "What have I got to offer that is so special?" He hurt her through comparisons, belittling, arguments and judgments.

This critic often holds some seed of truth. Through reflection, the constructive side of "Old Red Eyes" was revealed to his creator. When she tempered his negativism, he could present his truth without being destructive. Next to his image, she wrote ways that picturing him could help her:

He reminds me that I may not be Robert Frost or da Vinci, but neither is anyone else; if I do the best I can, I'm not perfect but at least I tried; I can use the questions he raises to make judgments and weigh possibilities rather than put myself down; I can learn from his criticisms and do better, rather than quit because I don't measure up to unrealistic expectations.

In her determination to do something about the critic, she advised herself:

Identify when the critic is operating and when I am; identify what is judgment and what is judgmental— a judgment, when examined, gives me something to reflect or act upon, while judgmental comments fill me with guilt and negation of self and offer little chance of change; remember that at least half of what I hear doesn't come from me but from someone else, some fear, some past hurt.

Clearly, working with the critic in image-making/ image-using revealed valuable information for this woman to apply to her daily life. So much is sacrificed to this negative voice that silencing it soothes many of the still-painful wounds of childhood and gives us a more positive and creative response to our lives.

When we work with the inner critic, our images are often dark and unnerving, such as *The Witch Woman* and *Disease* in Chapter One, but these are exactly the images that need embracing. If we are to gain insight into our-selves and others, we must discover the hidden side that clamors for expression. Remember, this critical voice is not our whole personality, but a part of us taken on from earlier experiences and reinforced over time. This voice originally guarded us from emotional risk ("If I don't paint, no one will be able to make fun of me"), but once we are adults this critical voice keeps us from much of the joy and excitement of life. What once might have been necessary protection is now destructive to our growth. As we become aware of this critical voice, we can learn to control it, helping our more capable, adult selves to emerge. Since the inner critic is an adaptation that we made over time, we can dismantle its negative power over us.

Our fear of the inner critic's accusations is spurred on by our competitive society. To free ourselves of socially-imposed (and self-imposed) competitive limita-tions to our individual development, we can begin by replacing competition with excellence, which "allows for and takes advantage of the emotional, more primitive side (good and bad) of human nature."[20] The inner artist

The Inner Critic

strives for excellence while the inner critic is an unmerci-ful competitor.

I knew a woman who dreamed of a dragon. She was frustrated because she couldn't draw it as she wanted to. Her inner competitive voice told her that her picture wouldn't be good enough. I encouraged her to color the dragon's energy, or what the dragon felt like to her. In this way she let go of her frustration, experienced the feeling of her dragon, and got in touch with what that energy might mean for her. She thought she wanted a picture of a dragon, while she really needed the dragon's energy. If we want pictures of things we can always find

Grove of Cypresses

them. But if we want the energy of the psyche we must trust the inner artist to produce the images that will lead us to it.

One way the inner critic blocks our connection to our own energy is to dismiss what we create with its opinion that the expression of emotions is not ''art.'' We can overcome this negation that resists creativity by reflecting on the works of great artists and reminding ourselves—and our inner critic—that art provides endless possibilities for expressing moods and feelings.

Vincent van Gogh's drawing *Grove of Cypresses* is provided here with a step-by-step exercise by which you can practice seeing with the artist's eye and ridding yourself of the inner critic's limiting voice. I use van Gogh because of his particular relationship to his own feeling side and his ability to express those feelings.

Seeing into Art and the Artist

For this exercise, sit in front of the van Gogh drawing for a minimum of ten minutes in silence, reflecting in the method described below. Read through the exercise before you begin and make a few written notes on your impressions when you finish.

The four basic steps are:

1. Think of anything that you might know about the artist. (Van Gogh was not a famous artist during his

Vincent Van Gogh, *Grove of Cypresses* (1889). Reed pen and ink over pencil on paper, 62.5 by 46.4 cm. Courtesy of The Art Institute of Chicago. Collection: Gift of Robert Allerton.

lifetime. He was a man who wrestled with the religious and philosophical issues of his world and found meaning in expressing what he grasped.)

2. Explore the drawing with your mind's eye to get a sense of its feeling tone. What mood do you feel? (As you look intently into this drawing, ask yourself: What sense of place is expressed? What energy comes out of the picture to meet me?)

3. Use a more critical attitude to examine how the piece was created. (Examining the piece closely, you will note that it is not a detailed drawing of cypress trees but a series of fluid lines and dots, creating an energetic and exciting image: a swirling dance that unites heaven with earth, and man with nature.)

4. Imagine the artist in the act of creating the piece. (Stay with the drawing; imagine van Gogh sitting in an open field on a bright summer day. In front of him are a piece of white paper and a dish of ink. He has a pen in his hand. He gazes pensively into the grove of trees in front of him. He notes the small peasant home nearby. With his eyes he embraces these trees, this house, the energy of life that he feels so passionately about. He wonders at his own relationship to all that his eyes behold. Amid the stillness, the pen begins to flow across the paper with bold intent—reflecting back the mood of this particular day, this style of peasant living, these many forms of nature, and the artist's sense of life's abundance.)

Note: These reflections are a model for you to use in working with other works of art.

In identifying with the artist at work, as a living being in a living world, we enliven our own inner artist and quiet our inner critic. In nurturing the inner artist, the part of us that can touch the spirit of great art, we touch the creative resources of our own being, and become more aware of the life around us. The inner artist brings our deeper, unknown aspects into consciousness. Expressed images provide the visual language that gives us new insight into ourselves and the surrounding world. Once free from the dominance of an overbearing, negative critical voice, the inner artist expresses and responds to the movements of life. This dynamic interaction of self-related-to-life generates a creative and healthy personality.

By creating personal symbols, the inner artist makes our unconscious images available to consciousness. Freedom from the inner critic allows the imagination to bring forth an ever-changing parade of images that can be worked with for self-awareness and further development of our personhood. One way to get past the inner critic is to choose against negative judgment and for creative expression. If we think we can't do something, we don't try, and we preserve our limited self-definition. We must assume that our unknown creativity is available.

When I work with a group I hand out art materials and ask people to make images of the subject we're dealing with. I assume that everyone is an image-maker and in turn everyone makes images. While some find this easier than others, everyone gives it a try. The effort stimulates the psyche's energy to express its unknown aspects. The unconscious speaks through colors and forms, bringing new awareness to the surface; thus, the images illuminate the problem being worked on.

The next exercise is designed for you to experiment with colors as part of the image-making process. It is meant to help you get more in touch with yourself and accept what you discover. Knowing that you are an individual and have no group influence while doing this, I suspect that you might skip this exercise because of the attitudes of your inner critic. I encourage you to give the art materials a try. The importance of overcoming the influence of the inner critic can never be emphasized enough, as it may be the most polluting voice in the psyche. To experiment with creativity is to begin to outgrow personal limitations.

Working With Color

Materials: drawing paper, graph paper, oil pastels or felt tip pens for strong vivid colors

Let the colors speak for themselves. Sit quietly and figure out your own color code. Remember that there are no "right" or "wrong" answers on this. Interpreting a color to mean a specific thing is not the point; what the color means to you is what's important.

Name the color for:
Thinking
Feeling
Sensation
Intuition
Creative growth
Gentleness
Outreach
Passion
Pain
Dryness
Despair
Confusion
Hope
Joy
Sadness
Anger
Practicality

Add any other moods or mindframes that you want to express.

Using what you've made as a color code, keep a record on the graph paper of your different moods for the next few weeks. See if there are daily/weekly/monthly trends or patterns.[21]

The following exercise is also designed to help increase your self-acceptance. As you do it, hold in your mind a conscious desire to keep the inner critic quiet and to embrace all that you reveal to yourself through your heart-image.

Heart Images

Materials: pen, pencil, drawing paper, colors

This exercise develops imagery of the heart. We think with our minds, but our thoughts are not always connected to our hearts. Working with images of what is in the heart can help unify thoughts and feelings. Search for what a heart really has in it. Accept what you find and make no judgments. As you learn to see and feel your heart more clearly, the power of the inner critic is diminished.

1. Draw an outline of a valentine heart on a piece of paper. Make it as large as the paper will allow — the larger the better.

2. Sit and gaze into the empty heart on the paper. Let the image of Heart fill your mind and body. Close your eyes and see it in your mind's eye. Feel your physical heart beating in your body. Breathe deeply, relax, and think and feel HEART.

3. Look into your own heart and see what you can discover about yourself. How does your heart feel? What does it hold?

4. Draw your experience of your own heart inside the heart on the paper. Develop it fully. Fill the heart with shapes or colors. Remember to include the dark as well as the light. Write down the words that come into your mind as you create the image.

5. Reflect on this image. Are there wounds in your heart that need healing? Are there unexpressed feelings that need to be released? Whatever you find, use the image to remind you of the complexity of your own heart and in turn the hearts of others. Let it teach you more about yourself and those around you.

As one man worked with his heart image he was shocked to discover that he was still carrying a broken

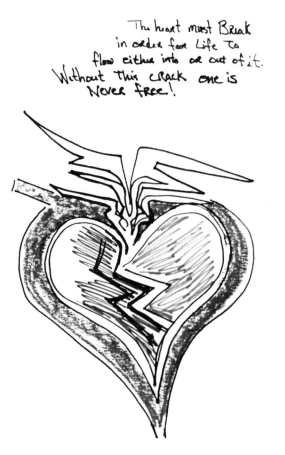

The heart must Break
in order for Life to
flow either into or out of it.
Without this crack one is
Never free!

The Broken Heart

heart from events long past.

As he examined his cracked heart he began to see that although emotionally painful, it also held the life-

Heart Image

eventually cut off the circulation of her positive feelings.

As we allow ourselves to experience the many dimensions of our own hearts and accept them into the image we hold of ourselves, the inner critic goes through transformation. The critic, like the shadow, has a positive possibility within it. This destructive voice can become constructive when brought into a balanced relationship with the rest of one's personality. I remember a client who had a dialogue with the inner critic in my office. We were both surprised to hear the critic say that he spoke so harshly because he couldn't get her attention any other way. When she agreed to consult with him, he agreed to stop using negative power to state his opinion. From then on this woman tried to think out what the critic wanted from her, and over time he changed from critic to valued companion. He originally had wanted to help her in some way, and her new method of reflecting on his messages allowed him to return to that role.

In facing the inner critic we have the chance to experience living without the self-negation that has become too much of our personality. We can relearn to value ourselves as human beings and enjoy the sense of celebrating who we are.

giving possibility of openness and exchange with others. The wound to his heart offered him deeper understanding of himself and others, and presented him with a sense of newly-found freedom: the freedom to be himself.

Another client making a heart image quickly saw the conflict she would be working with in therapy. One part of her heart was gentle and warm, as symbolized by the smile, while another part was being squeezed and distorted by the pressure of barbed wire. In examining her image, she realized that she was at a time in her life when she could go either way—expressed by the two arrows. She could break the wire to allow the expansion of heart or she could leave it there, knowing that it would

4

Image-making/Image-using

Whenever I ask new clients to create an image of what they are feeling or thinking, the first thing they usually say is, "But I can't draw." I assure them that a background in drawing is not necessary for the inner artist to create helpful images. Even abstract forms and stick figures are quite adequate self-expressions.

As people become less intimidated by the idea of image-making I suggest that they take pencil and paper and do the exercise below entitled "Drawing Upside Down" from *Drawing on the Right Side of the Brain*. It is a technique commonly used in teaching drawing; it might relax you to know that this exercise was recently used with wonderful success in my son's sixth grade class. If they can do it, so can you!

This is a particularly important exercise because of the delight you will have in completing a drawing and because of the additional understanding you will acquire about how beliefs work to control us. When we believe that we can't draw, we never pick up a pencil. In this exercise you will find that you can draw and only your belief that you can't is false.

Drawing Upside Down

(On the next page) is a reproduction of a line drawing by Picasso of the composer Igor Stravinsky. The image is upside down. You will be copying the upside-down image. Your drawing, therefore, will be done *also upside down*. In other words, you will copy the Picasso drawing *just as you see it*.

Before you begin: Read all of the following instructions.

1. Find a quiet place to draw where no one will interrupt you. . . . Finish the drawing in one sitting, allowing yourself about thirty to forty minutes—more if possible. Set an alarm clock or timer, if you wish, so that you can forget about keeping time. . . . And more importantly: *do not turn the drawing right side up until you have finished. . . .*

2. Look at the upside-down drawing for a minute. Regard the angles and shapes and lines. You can see that the lines all *fit* together. Where one line ends another starts. The lines lie at certain angles in relation to each

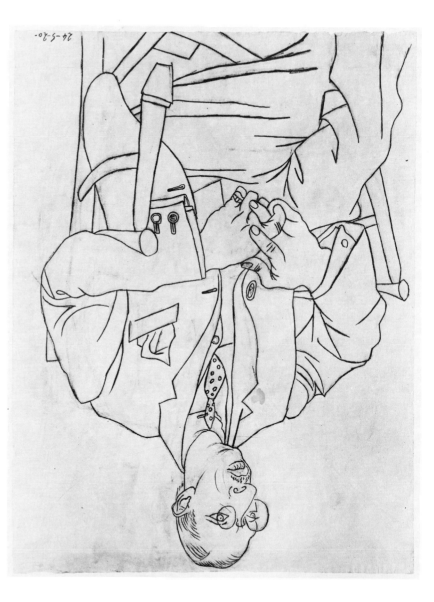

Portrait of Igor Stravinsky

Pablo Picasso, *Portrait of Igor Stravinsky.* Paris,
May 21, 1920 (dated). Privately owned.

other and in relation to the edges of the paper. Curved lines fit into certain spaces. The lines, in fact, form the edges of spaces, and you can look at the shapes of the spaces within the lines.

3. When you start your drawing, begin at the top and copy each line, moving from line to adjacent line, putting it all together just like a jigsaw puzzle. Don't concern yourself with naming the parts; it's not necessary. In fact, if you come to parts that perhaps you *could name,* such as the h-a-n-d-s or the f-a-c-e (remember, we are *not naming* things!), just continue to think to yourself, "Well, this line curves that way; this line crosses over, making that little shape there; this line is at that angle, compared to the edge of the paper," and so on. Again, try not to think about what the forms are and avoid any attempt to recognize or name the various parts.

4. Begin your upside-down drawing now, working your way through the drawing by moving from line to line, part to adjacent part.

5. Once you've started drawing, you'll find yourself becoming very interested in how the lines go together. . . .

Remember that everything you need to know in order to draw the image is *right in front of your eyes.* All of the information is right there, making it easy for you. Don't make it complicated. It really is as simple as that.

. . . Once you've finished and turned your drawing right side up, you'll probably be quite surprised at how well the drawing came out.[22]

After completing four or five upside down drawings you will see your skills improve and will be much encouraged by your artistic abilities.

Another way to learn that you can draw is offered in the next short exercise. In this exercise you have the additional benefit of being outside while practicing your drawing technique.

Life Around Us

Materials: pencil and paper (no eraser)

1. Sit outside with your materials and enjoy nature. A park bench, your front yard, any green space that you feel comfortable in will do. Breathe in the air, listen to the sounds, relax and take in all that surrounds you.

2. Turn your attention first to one feature of your environment, then to one aspect of that feature. You might look at "tree" and then examine a particular leaf on the tree, or start by seeing "plant" and concentrate on one blossom on the plant.

3. When you've focused your attention, begin to draw what you have chosen. Include all the details you can find—every little curve and line. Make no corrections, but draw the same thing many times, over and over, until you have a sense of looking into what you see. Don't worry about what the drawings look like. If you don't like one, draw another, and another. Keep drawing the same thing and learn all that you can. You'll find that one small leaf has a lot to say!

Life Around Us

Here's an example of drawing "Life Around Us."

Feeling more comfortable about drawing, you can now begin to discover your images. Once the eye of your inner artist is free to look for images, she will find them; you will be amazed to find how many are available.

You can begin by noting what you enjoy seeing. The flowers in front of the grocery store, the fog lifting off the water as you drive to work, the face of the man selling papers on the corner near your office—these are images. What you like or dislike tells you something about yourself. Other possibilities are movies, books, music, etc. All your senses take things in; take note of how you respond to what touches you. Discovering the images that have personal significance to you is primarily a matter of awareness.

Words—songs, poems, conversations—are also the material of image-making. If you don't consider yourself very visual, you will find it helpful to take the approach of finding your word images. The following exercise is designed to help with the exploration of the imagery available in words.

Word as Image

Materials: After reading through the exercise, choose those materials that seem best suited to the words around which you will be building an image.

1. Take a literary image that has meaning for you, such as a line from a poem or a quote from a book. Most of us have lines and phrases in our memory that easily come to mind.

2. Create an image that reflects the quote you have chosen. Express the experience of the words—what that phrase feels like or looks like to you. How would you put these words into a picture?

3. Sit in a relaxed manner and stare into the image that you have just created. Close your eyes and see the image inside your mind. Open your eyes and again stare deeply into your image. Let the line or phrase run freely through your head, over and over again. Breathe, relax, look at the image, listen to the words.

4. Make a few brief notes in your journal about what this image has to say to you. Write down the meaning you experience in these words and this image.

5. During the next week, let the image and words return to you as a meditative practice when you are walking somewhere, when you are feeling tense, or in any other way that you can include it in your daily activities. The following image was created in relation to a line from T.S. Eliot's *Four Quartets.*

Another source of images is your dreams, the best-known language of the unconscious. If you believe that you don't dream, be assured that you do; you simply don't remember dreaming. Put the suggestion into your consciousness that you will begin to remember your dreams. I also suggest that you write down or tape-record what you remember.

Recording your dreams in a journal provides important material for the inner artist. Keep your art materials near your bed. The next time you wake up with a dream image, put the image on paper before you start your day.

The following exercise will be helpful in working with dreams. You can read it now and apply it the next time you remember an image from a dream. Working

The Fire and the Rose Are One

with dream images increases your dreaming as well as your ability to remember them.

Working With a Dream

Materials: drawing supplies, such as oil pastels, chalk or felt tip pens and paper

Some dreams have particularly clear images in them, while others have strong feelings. Pick a symbol or a feeling from a dream that stands out in your mind.

1. Make an image of the symbol or the feeling of the dream. Concentrate on expressing the tone of the dream, not a picture of it.

2. When your image is complete, sit quietly and reflect on what you have created. Write down any words that come to mind. Relax with the image and get to know it.

3. Now ask your image questions. Form your own questions or simply ask it, "What do you have to teach me?" Be sure your questions can't be answered simply yes or no. Ask an open-ended question. Again, sit quietly and wait. Let the question float freely inside your head.

4. As an answer takes shape, write it down. Don't argue with what comes. Accept what is presented and try to learn what it might be telling you.

5. Keep this image in a place where you will see it in the next week and note any events in your life that seem related to this symbol. Check with yourself regularly to see if you are remembering the image and keeping it in your awareness.

I once worked with a man who was considering taking on a role of increased leadership and responsibility. As he struggled with this choice, he had two dreams. In the first, a woman guide gave him a necklace; she was to introduce him to a man who would be his teacher. In the second dream, three weeks later, he met a woman, the

The First Necklace

main speaker at a large gathering. He showed her another necklace, which a friend had given him. She told him that this necklace could move him through history. He replied that he had no idea that it was so important.

After the second dream this man made images of the two necklaces. As he drew these necklaces, he experienced his strength and ability to make the right choice about the issue he had been avoiding. He told me that when he was making the images he realized what the two dreams were showing him. He had been leaving an important matter undecided because he didn't feel

If you have spent time on the exercises "Feelings" and "Working With Color," you probably already have a new connection to the energy available through image-making around your emotions. If you tend to grasp things visually, you may find that numerous images come to you; it will be your task to discern which are the most important to work with. The feeling tone is always a good guide; also, any image that repeats itself is useful.

Be sure to write down any words or insights that come while you work on images. Write on the paper itself, next to the image, or in a separate journal. (You can use an artist's sketchbook as a journal and draw on one side of the open book while writing on the other.) When words are placed next to images, both take on a new and fuller meaning, carrying a deeper truth from the psyche. Some words flood out of the top of our minds, and some flow from the depths of our souls. It is the latter that we are looking for, as we probably know too much about the former.

At times when we don't remember our dreams, or there doesn't seem to be a particular image moving in us, we can turn to the library, where books are filled with the works of famous artists. In roaming through these books, we activate our imagination and the material of our unconscious. Our response to the images we meet helps us discover endless expressions of our deeper selves.

You can explore these unknown realms of the unconscious by using the following exercise.

A drawing called *Head of a Breton Peasant Girl* by Paul Gauguin is presented here for you to reflect upon and write about. In sitting quietly and hearing your inner

The Second Necklace

strong enough to say either yes or no. The dreams told him he had inner guides, teachers and leaders, but he only saw this when he drew the two necklaces. Once he had those images, he could use them to remind himself of his own unknown strength (the ability to move him through history) and his inner teachers (the man in the first dream).

Yet another resource for images is strong emotion: anger, sadness, happiness, confusion, or any intense feeling. Through art we can make these emotions accessible.

response to this image, you can experience what images evoke in your psyche. Follow the instructions given below and see what the Peasant Girl has to say to you.

Writing Around an Image

The only materials needed for this exercise are the drawing, some writing materials, and a comfortable place to sit.

1. Begin by propping this book up in a way that will allow you to look directly into the picture. Have your writing materials on your lap or somewhere within arm's reach.

2. Close your eyes and relax in the chair. Focus on your breath until you feel quiet and calm. Relax and clear your mind of thinking.

3. Now open your eyes and simply look at the image; don't think about it. Examine it with your eyes. What do you see? Examine it with your ears. What do you hear? It's speaking to you—telling you something about life. Let it speak as you gaze into its depths. Let its words float through your mind. Don't judge what you see and hear. Accept the words and ideas as they come. Don't hold on to any one thought; let each float past your awareness.

4. When you have absorbed the image, write down a list of the words and thoughts that passed through your mind.

5. Reflect on your words. Write a brief paragraph or two from the ingredients of your list. Your role is to create

Head of a Breton Peasant Girl

Paul Gauguin, *Head of a Breton Peasant Girl* (c. 1889). Graphite, black and red crayon, black wash on white paper, 224 by 344 mm. Fogg Art Museum, Cambridge, Massachusetts. Bequest — Meta and Paul J. Sachs.

some order from the words without being a judge or censor.

6. Read what you have written. It tells you something about yourself: how you feel, how you think, how you perceive the world around you.

Note: This exercise can be used with images from any aspect of life, but it will be most effective with those to which you respond strongly. If you know from the beginning that something speaks to you, positively or negatively, you are more apt to explore its meaning fully and take your responses seriously.

As we discover our images we want to express them and learn from them. They reflect knowledge of the unconscious world to us and thus bring a deeper and fuller meaning to our lives. Understanding images takes time, and it's useful to keep them in plain view where we can continue to relate to them and discover new aspects of what they might express. I advise my clients to keep everything that they create so that they will have a rich supply of images to return to and review.

Images often repeat themselves, but a long time can pass before they reappear. If we keep them accessible, they reveal patterns that we might not otherwise acknowledge.

An image that has appeared to me numerous times over the years is that of the Fool, as seen in Chapter One. Because this image repeated itself so many times I realized that I must learn more about what the Fool might mean. In researching the symbolism of the Fool I have learned that he is considered immortal, a wanderer, connected to both power and creative energy, and that "the fool encompasses all possibilities and can offer the inner counsel of fresh ideas and new energy."[23]

As we research ideas and concepts around images, we can also examine the ways in which these images are expressed. I illuminate my understanding of Fool by looking at depictions of fools and clowns created by such well-known artists as Picasso, Rouault, Shahn and Chagall. Fools teach me to stand on my head, walk a tightrope, do backbends and balance myself upon my animal nature. Psychologically, these are all stances that require fluidity and grace. An over-structured personality has little opportunity to participate in the dance of life, while the personality that is inclusive of the Fool turns many a joyous cartwheel.

Like the figure of the Trickster those parts of myself that seem a mistake, an embarrassment or an absurdity often turn out in the long run to teach me significant lessons.[24] The Fool expresses an archetypal image of an aspect of my psyche that is also available in the collective unconscious, teaching me that "to admit ignorance is the highest knowledge—the necessary condition of all learning" and that, as William Blake says, "If a man would persist in his folly, he would become wise."[25,26]

We can expand on our own images as we find archetypes in the works of artists, writers and scholars, and develop them through our inner artist; thus we develop a deepening, ongoing relationship to the energy of images on a collective level. I am cautious never to think that I completely understand their meaning. Doing so would rob them of their lifegiving possibilities.

In seeing these related images we can learn what they are trying to tell us. The unconscious does not present its images by accident, and if we don't get the message the first time we are often given other opportunities. The unknown parts of the psyche push into the light of consciousness and the inner artist links what we already know about ourselves with what we have yet to learn.

I know a woman who did a series of paintings, one of which was a nun with a masked face. This woman had little interest in structured religion and was not from a Catholic background, so a picture of a nun did not hold her interest. Because she had other images to work with, and it didn't seem important at the time, she placed it on a shelf. Many months later she reflected anew on her nun image and was delighted to discover in it an affirmation of her introverted aspect. An image that once seemed no more than a curiosity, when given time, became a yes-sayer to her deeper being.

Image-making is an organic process in the psyche and won't be rushed or controlled. It can be compared to a growing plant. One day we see the shoot; a week later the leaves appear; two weeks later a bud; and in due time a beautiful blossom. The images of the psyche must be related to in the same way—with the inner artist as our gardener.

This process as used here is not difficult if we let it happen—let it grow. It is a nonverbal form of communication, a way to connect to those aspects of life that are generally ignored. When I hear clients stop discussing a stressful situation by saying, "I can't remember exactly what happened," I offer them a piece of paper and crayons to see if they can show me how they feel. The

The Masked Nun

blocked feelings are released into the paper and memory returns. As they make images, they defuse a stressful situation by moving through the feelings rather than avoiding them. This can also be experienced outside the therapeutic setting; paper and colors on the dining room table provide what we need. I have a friend living in Europe who recently told me that if she hadn't taken the time to express her images and feelings while living so far from home, she wouldn't have made the changes needed to adapt to her new environment.

This use of image-making is a spontaneous response to a particular feeling or situation. It offers us a new way to connect to something in ourselves. By working with images we combine creativity with understanding to produce new dimensions of being that will facilitate our personal development. The image-making/image-using process at work in everyday life can be seen in the following case.

A client entered therapy to confront a high level of anxiety related to the pressures of her job and the tension of planning her upcoming wedding. Stress and self-negation impaired her ability to function well in her daily roles. She was beginning to believe that there was something wrong with her because she couldn't complete tasks, and that her life was out of her control.

When we began to work with her sense of being overwhelmed, I asked her to depict the part of herself that kept her from feeling able to handle her life. She instantly created a three-sided black box with a few colors inside it.

Her first response to the image was one of fear that it might develop its fourth side and completely lock her up. As she talked about the box she discovered it to be the voices and opinions of her family, which she internal-

The Box

ized over the years. The combination of two generations of family expectations were built up inside her. However, in looking more carefully she realized that these messages came from inside herself, not from her family. Now that the issues were clearly defined, she needed to find her deeper self beyond the negative internal voices.

I suggested that she make an image that would be the opposite of this box—what it would feel like to be free of these three black walls. In this image, the colors that had previously been inside the box were put together in a starburst pattern, creating an alive and compelling energy field that made her feel positive and

Starburst

excited. This represented the part of her that knew what kind of wedding she wanted, what would be best for her and how to handle any conflicts with her family that might come up.

The next step involved this client taking both images home and making them part of her awareness, thus reinforcing her insights. She could look at her situation and see whether the black box or the radiant form was dominant. She released much of her anxiety by examining the negative statements in her mind and finding that messages from the past no longer had power over her. She saw how she pushed herself too hard and how the colorful energy of the starburst was lost if she didn't take care of herself. She learned to support the energy she valued and release what threatened her. She learned to slow down, reflect, and act in ways that gave her the most satisfaction. By taking these opposed images seriously and working with them on a regular basis, she was able to resolve her internal conflict, coping with the demands of her job and preparing her wedding.

Work with images increases our life potential as we include the unconscious, the irrational, the right side of the brain, and the creative matrix of personality. The exclusion of opposite images is always a loss. Many images that we find in ourselves are frightening, but confronting them leads us to the discovery of the positive possibilities they offer.

If we dream of murder it does not mean that we will kill someone, but that we must include the capability of destruction in our self-awareness; that we sometimes feel murderous rage; that we have killed parts of our own souls by rejecting them. We may also harm others through thoughtlessness; threaten our bodies through neglect; and destroy the planet through over-consumption. As we become more sensitive to our actions, we can concern ourselves with creation rather than destruction.

We must also examine the opposite of our self-images. If we see ourselves as good parents, do we imagine our potential for being abusive? If we consider ourselves aware and insightful, do we include the part of us that is blind? Inclusion of such opposites leads to growth and an expansion of the imagination that is seldom taught, not easily learned, and must be diligently cultivated. Without it we are forever lost in an incomplete and misleading self-image.

The following exercise is designed to help in the difficult task of inclusion of opposites.

The Other Side

Materials: pen or pencil, oil pastels, and drawing paper

1. Begin by drawing a problem; look at "Drawing a Problem in Analog Form" in the Introduction. Let the problem come to mind and draw it with pencil or pastels. Add colors as you want. Draw how this problem makes you feel.

2. Look at the image and describe it to yourself. Write down anything you want about this problem and the way you've depicted it, but describe it as simply as possible, limiting yourself to short statements.

3. Ask yourself what is on the other side of this image. Visualize this opposite.

4. Name the other side of your problem; write that name on a new piece of paper and draw an image of it.

5. Write down the words that form around this image.

6. Place the two images side by side and observe how the second image (the opposite of the problem) could be helpful in dealing with the first image (the problem).

7. Write down your insights and return to them when this or a similar problem arises.

Once I was working with a woman who continually dismissed her own value and made herself feel unworthy. She recalled her dream of a dark-eyed witch staring at her. I asked her to draw this witch.

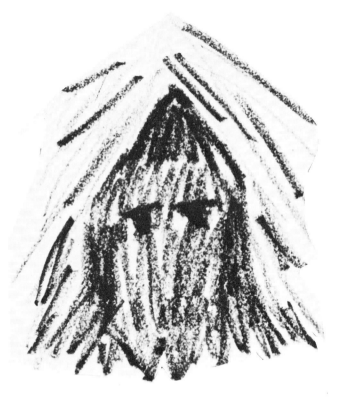

Witch

49

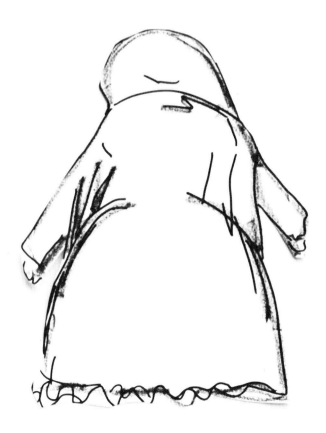

Earth Mother

We talked about her witch and how it terrified her. Then I asked, "What might be the opposite of this image?" She immediately created a line drawing that she titled *The Earth Mother*. She reflected on how this "earth mother" might help her deal with the hateful witch inside her. She could learn to like herself the way she was. She could nurture herself through positive reinforcement. Her image told her to "be at peace," reminding her that she didn't have to live in fear of the dark-eyed witch of her dream.

By reaching into the unknown parts of her psyche this woman acquired the positive energy to counterbalance her negative witch. We each have an inner witch that can destroy and devour us. We also have an earth mother that nurtures and strengthens. It is not psychologically healthy to live under the full control of either figure; giving the witch dominance means never feeling adequate, while living under the power of the earth mother alone can lead to a false sense of being the center of life.

We too readily accept these one-sided attitudes within us, seeing ourselves as either completely wonderful or terrible rather than realizing that the human personality is a combination of qualities. There are parts of us that must be dismantled and other parts that need to be strengthened and supported.

As we unify the opposites within us, we learn inclusion of the many aspects of who we really are; thus we grow toward psychic wholeness. In this newly-found sense of completion we reach into the depths of the psyche, finding there the transpersonal realm of the archetypes and the energy of the Self. Thus we build a life that is balanced within and without.

Connection to the Center

5

When we unify the opposites within us and work/play with the expressions of the inner artist, we find both creativity and the depth of universal aspects of the Self. There is much searching for this central depth, and the meaning and purpose it provides; Viktor Frankl calls this "the cry for something self-transcendent."[27] As a counselor I often hear this yearning as clients confide in me: "You might think I'm crazy, but sometimes I think there is something more that I am meant to do, something important, something for the world." It is this "something more . . . something for the world" that gives life a fuller meaning. Separation from the whole leads to emptiness and alienation. Connection to more than the personal level of existence is available as we explore the images of the psyche. This creative connection comes naturally to the inner artist.

We can also see the connection to the whole of life in the works of many great artists. If we spend time with Michelangelo's *David* or *Pietà* , or if we encounter van Gogh's *Crows in a Wheatfield*, we know that these artists have touched something of the divine, and that their work is significantly more than personal. With the guidance of the inner artist we encounter that part of the Self available to each of us. As Michelangelo saw the spirit of his creation in the stone as he worked, we too can experience the spirit that moves in and around our lives.

Often this spirit reveals itself through images like the following dream.

A woman in India becomes a reluctant Messiah. She is selling copies of a play that she has written. To those who buy she also gives something wonderful such as free entry to the play. It is very creative and loving on her part but she is overwhelmed by the response; she sees literally millions of people before her. She nudges a second woman and introduces herself, then she and the other woman walk away from the crowd. There is great pain in the two women as they climb a stairway, and women who follow them are also in pain. The Messiah figure instructs them not to fear the pain for it is God, and she says "We are of God in that pain and God is of us."

Woman With the God Center

The dreamer later used her picture of this woman with the God center to connect with the Divine in herself. To know God in one's pain is difficult, and this image was an important symbol for the dreamer during a long period of struggle.

A few months later the same woman was travelling in Europe and attended a museum showing of Marc Chagall's art work. She characterized the show as "wonderful" and was moved to send me a postcard of Chagall's *Pregnant Woman*. I couldn't help but associate the Chagall painting with her drawing. This woman's own image was reflected back to her through Chagall's work. She experienced the archetypal level of images as they are shared throughout society.

When thinking about archetypes and their influence on the psyche, it is always eye-opening to examine images. Over the centuries, from folk art to fine art, people around the world have created images of pregnant women and mothers with infants. As we are aware in our souls of the miracle of birth, the inner artist expresses this divine knowledge. Just as the "woman with the God center" is climbing the stairway, I see in the Chagall painting an expression of worship as the focus in the image is ascending. All the elements have an upward gaze; even the clouds appear to be in awe of this child-bearer. The child, already complete, waits to join the activity of daily living. The artist, inner and outer, knows that we are all carriers of this potential wholeness and bearers of the sacred aspect.

The Self must be carried and brought to new birth in the psyche of each of us, male and female. We must remember that this birth is sometimes glorious, as in Chagall, and sometimes painful, as in my client's dream. We must recognize and work with the Self in whatever archetypal form we receive it.

I have seen clients with a strong religious background who have lost their faith, feeling deserted by

God, because their image of God did not allow for pain and problems, leaving them without a religious resource in periods of crisis. To look deeply into one's transpersonal center reveals the presence of the Sacred that can be drawn upon even at times of conflict. We do not have to wait for the revelation of a dream to learn of such a Self. The inner artist can provide this deep connection, as the following exercise demonstrates.

Pathways to the Center

Materials: paper, pen, pencil, colors and journal

1. Draw a circle that fits the full size of your paper.

2. Sit quietly with your paper in front of you. Ask a question on this theme: What do I know of my own Center? Where is the Self in me?

3. Close your eyes. Focus on your breathing. Reflect on the question, not by looking for an answer but by letting the question sit inside you. Begin by feeling this center in your body. Breathe and hold the question.

4. When you feel that you're ready and have some experience of this center inside you, open your eyes and create an image in the circle. Don't think about it, but let it flow out of your hands. Hold the image and give it form and color on your paper.

Pregnant Woman

Marc Chagall, *Pregnant Woman*. Collection Stedelijk Museum, Amsterdam, on loan from Rijksdienst Beeldende Kunst. © ARS, N.Y./ADAGP, 1988.

5. When your image is complete you may want to write down a few words around the perimeter of the circle.

Note: This exercise can be done daily to help you understand the complexity of your own center. The image, as well as its colors and tone, will change each time you do it, showing you that the Self has multiple aspects and can never be set in a final definition.

The example shared below was created by a woman who worked on her own to express emotions through art

Mandala

materials. She didn't consider herself an artist, but she felt a release from strong emotional pulls by drawing with colors. One night she awoke with a mandala image in her mind's eye. The image remained so intense that she had to get up and put it on paper. She speaks of her image in the following ways:

> It was so completely spontaneous that I knew I could trust it . . .
> I expressed it exactly as I saw it.
> To change it in any way would be to impose my way over it.
> This image came from somewhere else inside me, not from where I think, and it wanted to be just the way it was.
> I can't explain it, but every time I look at it I feel good.

Trusting her feelings about the image, she turned the design into a piece of the "Ribbon Project," a peace demonstration in Washington, D.C. in August 1985. Friends who went to Washington that summer saw the design there; when the demonstration was over they brought it back to California and hung it in the hospital room at the birth of her second child.

The emergence of this particular mandala illustrates how images become part of meaningful living; the woman's central image is a statement for life and against destruction in herself and the world. The Self is expressible in an endless variety of forms. Although the mandala is the best-known and most thoroughly discussed example in Jung's psychology, we should remember that the

Self is limitless and is not confined to our definitions. The Self teaches us, and exploration of our personal symbols can direct us towards our divine nature.

The exercise below is intended to help in this exploration and to strengthen your relationship to the Self in your own psyche.

Personal Symbols

Materials: Choose anything you would like to use after you have read the entire exercise.

1. Begin by reflecting on who you are. Write ten short sentences that begin with "I am _____" and fill in the blank. As you reread your list, think about what form or image, other than human, could well describe you.

2. As your symbolic image takes shape in your mind, accept it; don't change it. A mouse or an inchworm is as significant as an eagle or a bear. Be true to yourself.

3. Choose the materials you'll use to express this form. You may want to draw, create a collage or make something out of clay; consider using natural materials such as twigs or stones, feathers or shells. Use your imagination.

4. Take your time and develop this image fully; if necessary work on it over a number of days. Give this project your full attention and make it as beautiful as you can.

5. When the image is complete, set it someplace special where you will see it often. Let it remind you of this unique aspect of yourself. Think about how you might

The Rose

learn more about your deeper nature by living in relation to this symbol.

Note: A day may come when this symbol holds less meaning to you. When this happens, put the image away and begin creating a new one.

The first image presented here is the expression of seeing oneself as a flower growing in the natural cycles of

The Hawk

shoot, bud and blossom. A meaningful personal symbol of life-death-rebirth has been beautifully created to speak to the living experience of the cycles of the psyche.

The second image is a collage created out of yarn, feathers, wool, a sand dollar and a drawing of a hawk. The imagemaker experienced herself as visionary, able to embrace a larger perspective. By creating her personal symbol she reminded herself of her more expansive nature.

As you use your personal symbols to connect to the divine Center, you may want to experiment with a variety of techniques for expressing what you find; this can be a life practice of unending possibilities. A client used his camera to create an image uniting the elements of himself that reflected his sense of Center while he arrived at a new awareness of the unity of nature. In turn he discovered for himself the root meaning of the word religion: *religare*, to bind back, or to bind together. In this binding of our lives, we find something of our own wholeness and healing. What was split apart in the psyche through our life experiences is reunited at the Center of our being.

Psychological healing takes place at different levels in the psyche: the level of healing personal problems and the deeper level of knowing the Self. Although reaching this greater depth requires more time and work than solving problems, it has a broader application. The images of the Self express a spiritual dimension of the soul. Through image-making/image-using in the deeper layers of the unconscious we can do the healing work of binding our souls back together while practicing the presence of God within.

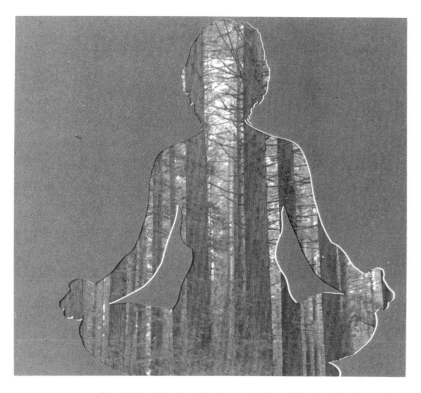

She Who Sits in the Forest/She Who Is the Forest

6

Obstacles to the Center

Although there are a number of psychological reasons why the ego chooses not to build the I-Self relationship, the primary one has to do with the issue of control. We like to have life our own way, and most of us have spent a long time developing who we are and how we live. We make most choices to benefit and maintain our ego-centered worlds. From birth, the human being tries to adapt the environment to meet his or her needs. Touching the Self may require us to adapt ourselves to meet the environment's needs. We resist such unusual demands. The I-Self relationship requires a revolutionary shift in our development. The Self becomes the center around which the ego moves. This is a healthy, but uncomfortable, limitation to the ego's control.

The most common block between the ego and the transpersonal Self is the fear of change. Staying in the life we know, even when it is dull, painful or without purpose, is often less frightening than stepping into the unknown. Vivid examples of this fear of change are seen in relationships where couples inflict pain on one another, pull apart, feel lonely, reunite, and then inflict pain again. A cycle of hurt and struggle ensues with no one willing to stop the abusive behavior by actually changing. Or we may be in a situation where we know that there is something regressive in our attitude that adheres to old, ineffective ways of doing things. We stay in uninteresting jobs or continue commitments that take up our time and leave us resentful and unfulfilled.

Change can be cultivated; self-reflection comes first, followed by action. If, for example, you are a person who has trouble making decisions, it is helpful to know why (self-reflection), but then you will have to practice making decisions (action) in order to change your behavior. The inner artist can help with the reflective work and she can even suggest what needs to be done, but it's necessary to take conscious action if insight is to become a living reality.

The inner artist can guide us in examining two elements of personality structure that regularly obstruct the way to the transpersonal Self.

The first involves looking at the childhood development that set in motion many of our current behaviors. For example, perhaps we treat our children as our parents treated us, or we treat them in the direct opposite of the way we were treated; in either case, our childhood experience taught us how to parent. Only by reflecting on what kind of parents we want to be, separate from our experience with our parents, do we stand a chance of becoming conscious about our own parental operating style.

There are obviously destructive childhood experiences like alcoholism, abuse and molestation, but many of us suffer from less obvious holds on the psyche. The overindulgent parent raises an irresponsible adult; the beautiful or talented child grows up to see him- or herself as the center of every situation. Such family dynamics, apparently easier to accept than overtly abusive situations, can be equally negative in their effects upon personality.

We do not examine our family background in order to blame others for our lack of development, but to release ourselves from the control of our old self-images. In this way we become open to new possibilities, and change becomes less fearful.

Use the following exercise to discover some of your own family patterns.

Family Portraits

Materials: Paint, chalk, crayons or oil pastels and lots of paper. Your materials need to be fluid for this exercise; have a number of sheets of paper available so that as the exercise grows you can just keep going from one sheet to the next.

1. Think back to childhood: the home that was most important to you, the members of your family, your pets, your neighbors, the things you liked or didn't like.

2. As the childhood images arise, draw that home and the family in it. Do you remember those school drawings that you did of "This is my home" or "This is my family"? Begin with a childlike drawing of that sort.

3. Be sure to include yourself in the picture. How do you fit into the family portrait? Were you the center? The outsider? Somewhere in the middle?

4. When the picture is complete, ask yourself about each family member. Who was smart, pretty, dumb? Who had the authority? Who was weak? Make up any questions you'd like to ask about the members of your family, including yourself.

5. Draw pictures of the different family members as you defined them in childhood. Don't let a voice inside you dismiss what you think about the family. Stay with whatever comes up in your mind and make as many images as you want.

6. Write a few words on the paper with the images so you will be able to recall what you were thinking as you created your family portraits.

7. Allow a little time to reflect on how the same family perceptions and definitions might be operating in your life today.

The Evaluator

A man who worked with the above exercise came up with the image titled *The Evaluator*. Reflecting on this image forced him to look at the part of himself that still carries on his family's ideas about the right way to behave. If he or anyone around him strays from the traditional family model, he senses that they will be judged by the powerful eye of this female figure. Her evaluation is, of course, always negative. He can never live up to her expectations; only when he finally says no to this negative authority can he begin to evaluate life for

himself.

In this case, *The Evaluator* emerged from the client's relationship to his mother, but it can as easily come from any other close childhood relationship. Such a judgmental figure is related to the inner critic, but operates more subtly and powerfully because of its source in childhood bonds. The family sets in motion our early ideal of love; if we are good enough, bad enough, smart enough, pretty enough—whatever "enough"— we will receive love. As adults we find ourselves still struggling to be "enough" to receive love; we also with- hold love from others, waiting for them to meet our expectations. These evaluations permeate life; the sins of one generation are passed on to the next—until someone is willing to change.

The second obstacle to reaching the Self is the image or face we present to the world. What mask are we wearing? Do people see us as good? Are we known for always getting things done? Do others turn to us for help? This mask, or persona, is only a partial image of who we really are. The danger of the persona is not that others see us this way, but that we want to be seen this way; we become identified with this face and neglect the person we might become. The persona becomes a screen through which we view the world and a defense against change. We can't accept anything that might disturb this face. We hide behind who we think we are rather than giving ourselves the chance to discover our more com- plex selves.

Experiment with the next exercise to learn some- thing about your persona.

The Persona as Mask

Materials: oil pastels and paper

1. Think about the face you present to the world. For some it is a smile, for others an angry mood or a rigid body stance. Whatever the mask, it serves to shape your life.

2. In what ways do you distance people or events from your inner self by wearing this mask?

3. With the oil pastels, create an image of your persona. Make a mask of the face you wear most of the time.

4. Examine your mask and write down the different ways in which it protects you. What parts of yourself are you keeping hidden?

5. Re-examine the image you've made and consider the value, and the cost, of carrying this mask everywhere you go. What would happen if you left it at home once in a while?

6. When you are out in the world, let the image created in this exercise come to mind. Ask yourself if you are wearing your mask and if you could let it down. Make a conscious choice to remove the persona whenever you can. Also be conscious of your choice to wear the mask so that you won't be fooled into thinking that your persona is your personality.

An example of a mask/persona is presented here. The words that spoke to the image-maker from this image were "I try to maintain my cool, but . . ." If you look deeply into this face, attractive as it is, you will see a sadness reflected in it—a sadness that speaks of the unlived life locked behind the strong face. Maintaining one's cool has a price; this mask has one blind eye and a silenced mouth.

Early childhood impressions and images of the persona often overlap. Ordinarily, we create a persona that fulfills some childhood imagery, some ideal of who we should be. These old structures must be broken down so that the psyche can grow into its own nature.

Along with the inner structures there are outer, lifestyle structures that present roadblocks to the center. The "too busy" syndrome leaves little time for inner work. It is only when we decide to devote time to the inner artist and her creativity that we can make the self-discoveries discussed in this book.

Probably the most important resource for facilitating image-making is a quiet, uninterrupted time in which to do it. Thirty minutes once or twice a week is not a great deal of time, but it is important to protect ourselves from the activity and noise of daily life. Too frequently, we allow ourselves to be bombarded by meaningless images and noise at the expense of our soul images and our true voice.

Silence helps us reach the "stillpoint" in the psyche from which both words and images emerge; in this silence we may find them united in full expression. James Hillman says: "Man is primarily an imagemaker and our psychic substance consists of images; our being is imaginal being, an existence in imagination. We are indeed such stuff as dreams are made of."[28] We come to realize that in the beginning is not word, but image. We have yet to speak the visual language that could bring greater self-fulfillment. We must invest the time and energy needed to contact and develop the images that lie restlessly below the surface of our awareness.

When we have learned to work in silence to discover our images, we are ready to make these discoveries concrete. In the two exercises in this chapter, for example, we can anticipate such action. Acting on our new knowledge is as important as the images themselves and the understanding that they afford. Insights without action toward change are merely interesting concepts that leave us observing our own negative cycles, still open to psychological destruction.

Actions do not need to be huge or dramatic but they must be grounded in specific steps. In the family portrait exercise above, the man could take several different steps, such as doing something which he knew his internalized parent (and possibly his real parent or parents) would condemn. It could be big, like spending money on a luxury vacation (the parent always saves), or small like buying a pink shirt ("How unmanly!" the parent exclaims). He could stop evaluating other people by the same standards that ruled him; he could stop trying to be perfect; he could let himself be worthy of the love of those around him.

We can overcome the obstacles that keep us in shallow layers of personality and reach into the depth and richness of the divine Self that desires life in the world. Religious experience is not a monopoly held by

Mask

the mystic; the divine is in the depths of every soul, waiting to be discovered, embraced and put into action.

Being of Light

7

Serving the Whole

As we overcome the obstacles to the center, the divine spark in each of us is revealed through image-making/ image-using. But such revelation is only the beginning. Integration goes further, bringing this newly discovered awareness into daily life. Open to change, we continually uncover images that encourage our future development.

One such image is *Being of Light*, discovered through a woman's writing and meditation. She didn't see herself as a "being of light," but was encouraged by the image to let this Being shine forth. While some voices in the psyche negate us, others remind us that we are the "light of the world." These archetypal images are brief glimpses into the depths of the Self in which we are meant to live.

A wonderful example of the ability to gaze into the unknown Self is the work of William Blake. He believed his art to be inspired by God and referred to his creative activity as "divine imagination." In his drawing *The Deity, From Whom Proceed the Nine Spheres*, Blake shows us the illumination that suffuses all life. The radiant circles in his drawing and the central circle in *Being of*

Light can be seen as mandalas — symbols of wholeness. Throughout history, images of life's divine nature have presented themselves for expression.

Unfortunately, these images can be lost as quickly as they are found. Blake created images throughout his life, never neglecting his divine imagination. Like Blake, we must have passion for the spirit of life and creativity that wants expression through us. The Self as part of consciousness does not live on its own. The danger in images of the Self is that we may think of them as something that we achieve, a fixed goal, rather than an ever-changing, dynamic process in which we constantly participate.

In my therapeutic practice, I have found examples of the barrenness of nonparticipation among addictive or depressive clients. In the case of addiction, images are evoked and observed but then abandoned. The person finds the image "enlightening" at the time of the experience but soon, feeling lonely and disconnected from anything meaningful, resumes his/her addictive behavior.

I have seen depressed clients who had dreams as

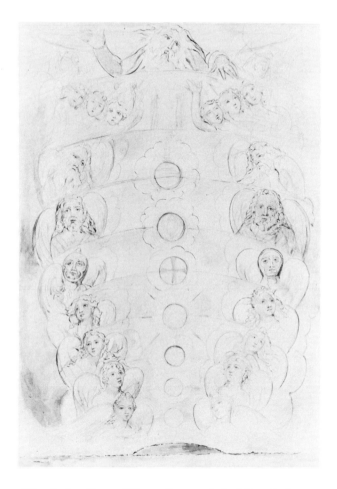

The Deity, From Whom Proceed the Nine Spheres

William Blake, *The Deity, From Whom Proceed the Nine Spheres.* Courtesy of
Ashmolean Museum, Oxford.

visionary as the art of Blake, but who dismissed them as
bizarre or unimportant. Rather than develop an image,
these clients may write it down (if they remember it),
read it to their therapist (if they think of it), then
promptly forget it. If unattended, the healing power of
the image is dissipated while the client remains depressed
and finds therapy of no benefit. The image emerges from
the unconscious, presenting an opportunity for contact
with the sacred—an attempt of the psyche to heal itself.
But if we're unwilling to know our inner nature, we limit
our chance for healing.

To live up to our images of the Self, we must
actively acknowledge and respond to what they tell us.
We attain creative living through ongoing relationship to
our deeper selves, bringing our psychic complexity into
fruition. We must not ignore, manipulate or misuse the
rich and powerful images of the psyche.

In coming to know our images we will find an inner
guide in relating to the Self. A woman who was exploring
the feminine side of the source of life found that wisdom
was available in the image of a "She-God" that she was
making. She wrote:

> I asked this image how I could grow to be more like
> her. I do not know many women who have those
> qualities that I admire: softness with strength, ten-
> derness without sentimentality, gentle wisdom, quiet
> self-confidence, warmth and openness. She gave me
> sound advice: "Honor your introversion, your ex-
> pressive arts. Follow the music and the gardening;
> follow your body, your senses. Make life more sen-
> sual for eyes, ears, touch. Lure yourself away from

by her "She-God" she discovered much about herself:

> I found that I had more choice in the way I spent my time, pushing aside the inner parent who told me I should do something "useful" and staying more with the impulse of the moment—listening to what my body felt like doing. It is not always easy for me to "indulge" myself in this way. Though I may consent intellectually, it has taken me a long time to realize how much I have been driven by a lopsided sense of duty to attend to outward demands.[29]

We also risk losing contact with the Self if we think we have "arrived," are "enlightened," or have achieved some special consciousness. The Self is not something we can take credit for; it works through us (possibly what Blake meant by "divine imagination"). It is not to be taken lightly, and requires evaluation and attention. We always need to check on the dangers of spiritual inflation. Seeing ourselves as wise or all-knowing, having all the answers, and thinking that we are more conscious than others are signs of this inflation. There is always the danger of confusing the God-Center with our ego, thinking "I am the center" or "I am God." As Shunryu Suzuki says:

> If you think that God created man, and that you are somehow separate from God, you are liable to think you have the ability to create something separate, something not given by God. For instance, we create airplanes and highways. And when we repeat, "I create, I create, I create," soon we forget about God. This is the danger of human culture. Actually to

She-God

ideas, television, politics. Be with yourself more, not with what people would have you be. Experiment. Turn off thinking and programming. Feel nature, food, light, darkness, rain, sun, moon. Walk, swim, sleep and dream; then work with what comes out of these."

As this woman tried to integrate the teachings given

I and the Village

create with the "big I" is to give; we cannot create and own what we create for ourselves since everything was created by God.[30]

I once heard a well-known therapist speak bluntly about the risk of focusing on creativity with clients. He told of a woman who while in therapy began to make pottery as an expressive outlet. She became so taken with her artistic endeavor that she left her husband and children without resolving any of her conflicts, and went on to make an abundance of mediocre pots. We must remember that creativity can be a source of ego-inflation, centering upon ourselves as creative persons, or thinking of our creations solely as reflections of ourselves. We easily forget that creation indicates our connection to the Whole.

A marvelous expression of this connection can be seen in Marc Chagall's painting *I and the Village*. It illustrates the artist's relationship to the environment of his childhood, and his attitude toward life. The face in the painting is that of Chagall himself. The cow was a creature he knew well. He said of the cow: "...the cow in our yard, with her milk as white as snow, the cow who used to talk to us."[31] Growing up in a peasant family, Chagall knew the interdependence of life. Many of his paintings depict these connections among human, animal, plant, community and the divine.

I and the Village expresses interconnection and interdependence by its use of the line that connects the

Marc Chagall, *I and the Village* (1911). Collection, The Museum of Modern Art, New York. Oil on canvas, 6′ 3 5/8″ by 59 5/8″. Mrs. Simon Guggenheim Fund. Photograph © 1988 The Museum of Modern Art, New York.

eye of the cow to the eye of the man; through the circular form that unites the various images in the painting; and through the radiant plant held in the artist's hand. This painting challenges us to reflect on our relationship to life around us. What do we know about the Whole? What can Chagall teach us? Do we know the value of animal and plant life as he did? Do we see the stardust that vibrates around the flowers as we pick them?

Chagall was a man of imagination, dreams, and visions. The artist can express the unity of life's aspects through the more irrational elements of his personality. The inner artist can guide us in the image-making process and the integration of the Self into our personality and worldview.

It is important to stay in touch with our part in the whole of things. We are not the image (we are not the Self); the image is part of us. If we focus on our images as the Center itself we limit the possibilities of how the Self might want to come into being. Again we make rigid what is meant to be fluid. We must be willing to explore, create, and grow in consciousness while accepting the mystery and irrationality of what we uncover. It is important to be creative, and what we create is significant, but it is not the end in itself.

It may seem strange to have written so much about the inner artist and image-making and then describe them in negative terms. Everything contains its own opposite and we must remember the dark side of this process. If we allow the process of creativity to take over, we risk being lost in the illusory power of images and symbols. Imagination is wonderful but it isn't the entire psyche. One aspect of this illusion can be seen in the widespread attitude that artistic talent is something special, available only to a privileged few, allowing outrageous behavior from artists. Somehow it is acceptable when the artist leaves her husband and children to pursue her art, but what do we think when the ordinary citizen packs up to find his own place? The former is a creative genius while the latter is a bum. Creativity and daily living go hand-in-hand. In the words of Suzuki: "If we are aware that what we do or what we create is really the gift of the 'big I' then we will not be attached to it, and we will not create problems for ourselves or for others."[32]

We work with images for the discoveries they bring us. We must also release them for the freedom to go on. In the Navajo sand-painting ceremony, the medicine man creates the painting and calls upon the spirits. Once the painting has done its work, he erases it. In the same way, we must let go of our images. As Lao Tsu says:

The Tao that can be told is not the eternal Tao.
The name that can be named is not the eternal
  name.
The nameless is the beginning of heaven and
  earth.
The named is the mother of ten thousand things.
Ever desireless, one can see the mystery.
Ever desiring, one can see the manifestations.
These two spring from the same source but differ
  in name;
This appears as darkness.
Darkness within darkness.
The gate to all mystery.[33]

We work with the manifestations while holding to the mystery. We honor and remember mystery through symbols and images while living in the world connected to the Self. In this way our lives—our manifestations—contribute to ongoing creation.

Creativity serves not only the individual but the whole of life. Just as great artists have contributed to the world, our inner artist and our personal healing symbols and images can aid in the healing of all life. We begin with ourselves. Everyone suffers from some form of wound: physical, psychological or spiritual. Coming to terms with personal wounds frees our energy to work at the world's wounds. Through image-making/image-using we stimulate personal healing and liberate our energy for larger life-giving possibilities.

To discover the impact that the inner artist can have on your own wounds, work with the following exercise as a way to bring healing energy to the pains and struggles of everyday living.

Healing a Wound

Materials: Keep them simple. A pen or pencil, some paper and your colors will do.

To begin, reflect on some wound in your life, some unresolved issue: hurt feelings, a broken heart, illness, the need for forgiveness or a harsh God image.

1. Identify the problem. Create an image that expresses this wound. (You may want to reread "Drawing a Problem in Analog Form" in the Introduction, page 5.)

2. When you have drawn the problem, look into the image and let the question "What is needed to heal this particular wound?" float around in your mind. Don't attempt to formulate an answer. Wait for another image to present itself.

3. Create the healing image that comes to mind. Allow it to change as you work. Don't plan the image. Let it form itself. Develop this image more fully by adding color. When the image seems complete, go over it again and again with color. Keep making it stronger until you are satisfied that this image can help you.

4. Place your first image (the wound) next to the second image (the healer) and reflect on what they have to tell you.

5. You may want to write in your journal about what you will need to do for the healing aspect to continue to grow and support you.

Note: It is very important not to define healing as "making the wound go away". Healing is often something that comes out of the wound itself and our relationship to it. The desire to have the wound gone leads to our defining what healing "should" be rather than staying open to what healing might really be.

In looking into wounds we must overcome our own resistance to facing the pain in our psyche. Resistance is a common response that keeps us from change. I had a client who regularly used the expressions "I don't care" and "it doesn't matter" to resist looking deeper into herself. As she realized that she must face the pain of childhood wounds, she began to use the inner artist to overcome her resistance and express her long-buried experiences.

In therapy she brought up the memory of a dream that had haunted her when she was four years old; she had to pass through it every night before she could sleep soundly. In it, she and her mother were at a train station. Her mother left her sitting on a bench and went off to purchase something, perhaps tickets for their journey. The child knew that her mother would never come back for her. Deep sadness filled this woman as she talked about her childhood dream. She drew a picture of it and called it a "sepia dream" because it had no color.

As we discussed the image of the abandoned child, she revealed that when she was four years old her nurse married and moved to another town. This nurse had been her "mother figure" since birth. No one in the family considered what this loss might mean to the little girl and she was left to cope by herself with her feelings of abandonment. Her adjustment was the dream that she had to endure "like a test" every night. She also learned to say "I don't care" or "It doesn't matter" in order to come to terms with this deathlike loss.

In allowing herself to re-experience this childhood wound and create an image of it, this woman brought the wound more fully into consciousness. As she drew, she felt that the wound still bled and needed attention, so she added a red ring around the outside. Letting the wound bleed freely, she thought, might help it to heal. So she added drops of blood to her image, then experienced the blood and pus flowing onto a second and a third piece of

Sepia Dream

paper. The image began to change; the blood and pus flowed over a cliff like a waterfall. Colors streamed into the river and a tree sprang up: a many-colored, lifegiving tree that came out of the wound and healed it at the same time.

As this woman kept her images alive, she realized that the attitude of "I don't care" had vanished. After forty years her caring was allowed to flow forth once more. Through embracing the images of her inner artist

Tree

this woman began to experience personal transformation.

As you work with images, the inner artist facilitates the movement of healing and change. Not only will you feel better about yourself, but you will see more clearly your relationship to life around you. You will no longer be dominated by your personal issues as the center of the world. Personal and collective are in exchange; all forms of healing contribute to the Whole. Through the experience of wounding and healing, compassion is developed. Out of compassion comes the desire to respond to situations that are more than personal.

Citizen of New Day, Woman With the God Center, She Who Sits in the Forest/She Who Is the Forest, Being of Light, Mandala, She-God and *Tree* are all examples of this personal healing that connects to the world's healing. These images are personal to their creators while archetypal and transpersonal in their imagery. The image of the whole earth as seen from space holds out the possibility of collective healing because it evokes our appreciation of this beautiful planet and challenges us to meet her needs.

As wounds are healed and the Self emerges within us, we find an inner desire to serve creation. All creation is part of the Self, weaving together the multiple aspects of our personality into the larger picture of family, community, work and world. In this weaving we become healthier—more integrated in our own psyches and into the world. We can become part of a new consciousness directed toward world transformation. As James Douglass says:

> The kingdom of Reality will be like lightning striking in the east and flashing far into the west when that hidden, latent energy of the unconscious Self which is God and humanity has been opened by sacrifice and allowed to surface into a conscious flash of truth, force of oneness manifested in a spiritual chain reaction . . . [34]

The inner artist can help us find this world-transforming energy. We must learn to trust her. As I was working on writing the conclusion to this chapter, two images appeared in dreams to show me what was needed.

Both images are statements about how life works; I developed the statements into exercises. The first is called *Perspective*.

Perspective

Statement: The circle is the planet Earth. The dot is a person. We are each one small pinpoint of life on this planet. The line extending from the dot is what that person is putting into the world.

Exercise

1. Fill in this circle by writing down what you've been putting into the world this week. How have you spent your time and your energy? Have you been angry? Did you resolve it? Have you been hurt? Did you heal it? Did you create something? Did you say "Thank you"?

2. Reflect on the value of your actions. Think about your contributions and what you might need to change for the coming week.

Note: We can also reflect on this issue from the perspective of each person on planet Earth being one small dot and think of all the energy that might be available for world transformation through these collective dots.

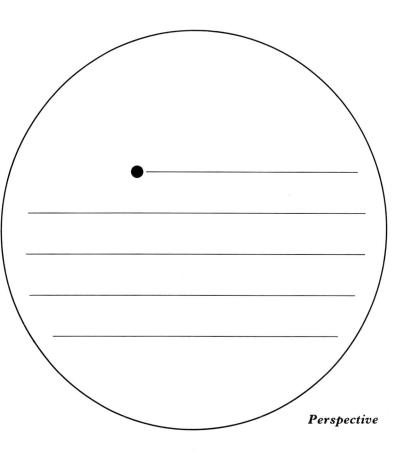

Perspective

The Crystal Weaver

The Crystal Weaver

Statement: When we have finished a project, we give it to a woman who will weave it into a beautiful pastel crystal. She is the Crystal Weaver and her work is to weave our actions into the greater whole of life.

Note: This is one of those irrational statements provided by the unconscious for us to come to terms with. We have no idea how anyone could weave a crystal, yet we must be willing to give what we create to this weaver to do her work. The language of the unconscious is often symbolic and consciousness must work to include what it does not rationally understand.

Exercise

1. Choose to bring some personal situation to the best resolution you can. Finish a project you've been leaving unattended; you could work at the exercise in this chapter titled "Healing a Wound," make an apology for some action you know was inappropriate, etc. You cannot expect to resolve all things, but you can direct your energy toward resolution and then accept the result.

2. Be resolved on the issue you have chosen. Let it be complete as it is and imagine turning it over to the Crystal Weaver—some force larger than yourself.

3. You can also use ritual to release the energy invested in the issue. Create an image of the issue you chose to resolve, then ceremonially burn it. As you watch it burn, fill your mind with the idea of releasing it into the hands

The second image is called *The Crystal Weaver.* Read and reflect on this image, then see where you can use it in your daily life.

of the universe. It is no longer yours to worry about or try to control.

An important ingredient of letting go is to acknowledge that there is a larger movement to life than you can know. We have all experienced thinking about someone and having that person appear on our front step in the next hour. We say "I was just thinking about you." We have a sense that something has happened, but we have no clear explanation for it. This is a simple illustration of how we know we don't control the events around us, yet are left to wonder how we might affect them.

As I reflected upon my dream of the Crystal Weaver I wanted to understand more clearly what this figure might mean. Using the method described in Chapter Four under the exercise "Working With a Dream," I began by painting her, then asked her, "What do you want to teach me?"

She responded by telling me: "You must remember that the development of individual wholeness is profoundly connected to the larger wholeness of the universe, and I, the archetypal feminine, the great mother, the goddess, am the weaver of those connections." She revealed that she needs our human contribution to help provide the materials of her weaving, and that if we do not develop our unique individual qualities her creation will be diminished.

The Crystal Weaver reminds me that we must do all we can to bring about the next level of personal and planetary transformation. We are responsible for being aware of what we put into the world, resolving the conflicts of our lives, and releasing what we accomplish to some larger force of life. As the inner artist helps us connect to the sacred Self within, we must encompass the complexity of what this Self might be. Although it is ours to discover in the depths of the psyche, it is also much more vast, surrounding us in all life at all times.

I cannot predict how world transformation will come about. Nonetheless, a model that draws forth individual healing can be generalized and have its effect on a larger scale. When we are healthier, we will create a healthier world. A tapestry of connections is in the weaving and we each have the opportunity to contribute our small but significant thread. As Rilke imagined:

> . . . and the smallest event unfolds like a fate, and fate itself is like a wonderful, wide fabric in which every thread is guided by an infinitely tender hand and laid alongside another thread and is held and supported by a hundred others . . .[35]

8

Image Work in Therapy

In addition to using the exercises in this book, an individual can work effectively on the journey to the Self by initiating a relationship with a psyche—or soul—therapist. The client and therapist who apply image-making/image-using to psychotherapy enter the realm of active imagination, fantasy and visualization. The advantage of creating images during therapy is that the material of the psyche takes concrete form. Thus, it is more than talked about; it is seen. The mind's eye reveals newly-discovered insights to client and therapist alike.

The therapist does not have to be an art therapist but must respect the dreams, symbols and images that emerge from the unconscious side of personality. The unconscious is an invaluable resource for awareness, growth and healing. It contains not only our forgotten past, but also holds "all the material that has not yet reached consciousness."[36] To leave the unconscious untapped during therapy is an injustice to the possibilities of human personality.

Image-making/image-using affords access to whatever might be in the vast reservoir of the unconscious.

Although training in the interpretation of unconscious content is not obligatory, the therapist's task is to guide clients toward understanding, respecting and integrating as much of themselves as possible.

The traditional analytic approach to working with the unconscious suffers from two major limitations. First, few people in the helping professions are trained in working with archetypal psychology. Second, few clients have the time or money to invest in years of frequent therapy sessions. Therefore, long-term psychoanalysis, however valuable, is available only to a small percentage of the population.

Short-term therapy, such as crisis intervention, behavior modification or systems theory, benefits the client, but often neglects the unconscious. As a result, many people spend four to six months in counseling to make their lives function better, only to turn around and repeat their destructive patterns. Quick methods of therapy, although less costly, may treat only the surface level of a person's difficulties. I suggest finding a therapist who works with the unconscious and is interested in creativity, but who does not expect that clients spend years in therapy.

The techniques described in this book can easily be adapted to the average therapy session. Image-making can be used effectively in ten to fifteen minutes of a regular fifty-minute hour. The only materials needed are a medium-sized drawing tablet that can be held comfortably on the lap, a box of oil pastels, and a pencil or pen.

A major function of the image-making/image-using process is to break through habitual patterns of perception, thought and behavior. People come to therapy because their normal, habitual mode of operation is no longer satisfactory. The inner artist can create images that will help in the formation of new behaviors. Both client and therapist are often astonished to see the images that arise in response to a question or a simple set of instructions. Often what is not available because of a lack—or an excess—of words can be released in a motion of the hand and a splash of color.

My Room

To illustrate the impact of image-making, I asked a client to recall working with images both in a therapeutic setting and on her own. She wrote:

I started therapy because I felt walled up, almost entombed in my marriage. During my first session I described my feelings of desperation, of "starving to death," and the way my life felt inauthentic, dull and gray. Between the first session and the second, I had a long dream from which I awoke with feelings of suffused

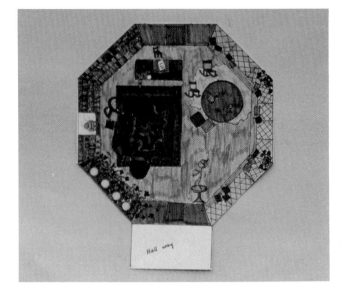

My Room: 1

and radiant warmth, as though a healing had taken place. In working through this dream during my second session I described the dream; it involved my discovery of a room at the end of a long hall in my house. This room was vague and shadowy as I passed through it. It did not seem particularly important to me but my therapist suggested I draw it.

In my first drawing, the room was octagonal with doors on opposite sides. One half of the room was heavily masculine, with tufted red leather sofas, a heavy "judge's" desk, bookcases and some scraggly houseplants. The other half of the room was light and feminine: There were large windows that I could open; there

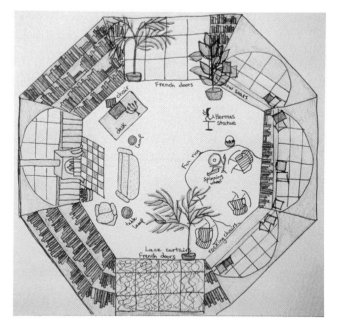

My Room: 2

were fur throws on the marble-tiled floor and window seats with pink and purple silk pillows. I also saw a spinning wheel, baskets of yarn, a low table and a harp. Flower baskets hung in the windows. I drew all this in about twenty minutes in my therapist's office.

Later the same week, I tried to make a better drawing of the room, but I found to my surprise that it had changed a bit in the interim. In the "masculine" half, the bookcases no longer contained only books but now held all sorts of carved African heads, fertility sculptures, ancient scrolls, ritual objects such as cups and incense burners, and directly behind the desk, dozens of dark blue bottles with strange labels on them. The desk had changed from a "judge's" desk to an ordinary wooden desk. On it was a half-finished letter with the greeting "Dear Emma." I also saw a magician's hat with silver stars and a child's "Sno-ball"—a glass globe with snow swirling around a tiny village. The red leather sofas had disappeared and in their place was a chaise longue with Oriental carpets and pillows thrown over it, flanked by two fat, padded velvet armchairs. The scraggly plants were replaced by a neat row of African violets. This side of my room now resembled a place where Jung might come for consultations.

The other, "feminine" side of the room remained much the same except for a couple of alterations; two rocking chairs had appeared next to the low table and the harp had disappeared. In its place was a lifesize statue of Mercury on a three-foot pedestal. Just as I was completing my drawing, a woman with the head of a bighorn sheep, dressed in a Greek toga, appeared and sat in one of the window seats. My conversation with this woman (which I wrote down as it occurred) became my first active imagination.

In the weeks that followed, I visited this room two or three times a week and recorded my conversations and adventures there. At first, it was quite crowded— sometimes there would be four or five personages, not always human, in the room and I found it hard to write my notes fast enough. It seems many people from "the other side" had been waiting for my attention. There were riotous parties with drumming, singing and dancing; babies were born; quiet conversations occurred. My guests brought me gifts, admonitions, comfort, laughter. I never knew whom I might encounter but I always began the same way: I walked down the hall of my house in my imagination, stood before the door and said out loud, "Whoever is within, I am ready to meet you and I trust you will not hurt me." Then I would open the door and enter. My visitors have astonished and delighted me.

After the third or fourth week, I discovered that my guests would sometimes pop into my mind while I was washing dishes or caring for my children. One day I suddenly knew that Toni Wolff, Jung's friend, was in the room. As soon as I could, I "went to my room" and did an active imagination with her because I was afraid she might leave. However, since then, I have learned that I can promise to come when I am able and my guests will wait. As I have become more sensitive to the process of using my room, I can now recognize a subtle insistent feeling which tells me that someone is waiting for me. If I ignore this feeling, sadness and fatigue overtake me until I return there.

In working repeatedly with the image of my room I have learned that the process of visiting it will continue to evolve in ways I can neither anticipate nor control. I have now made it my practice to draw something from each visit—perhaps the memory of a gift or a face—or some alteration in the room, as it seems to change continuously. Drawing various aspects of my visits gives me the feeling that these encounters are substantial, living realities which I can experience with my whole body, not just my mind. Often they are as real to me as the expe- riences of my daily waking life. Although my drawings are technically crude and childlike, they hold for me a numinous glowing beauty, and they seem to feed that part of me which was starving when I first entered therapy.

Depending upon the therapist's theoretical frame- work, the image of this room and its contents could be worked with in a variety of ways. The importance of the imagery is not in its interpretation by the therapist, but in its lifegiving energy for the client. When the client learns to use this energy, interpretation can follow as the images fit into his or her life. The therapist's primary role is not to interpret but to guide the client in connecting to the imagery of the unconscious and to stimulate maxi- mum personal and transpersonal development.

Image-making connects the conscious and the unconscious through what Jung called the "transcend- ent function," a psychic development that can "make the transition from one attitude to another organically possi- ble, without the loss of the unconscious."[37] Just as the inner artist can be instrumental in linking the two major dimensions of personality, so can the psychotherapist.

This double model of the psyche is similar to the design of the brain, whose two hemispheres are held together by nerve tissue that facilitates communication between them. The transcendent function connects the complex multiple aspects of the personality. A person who functions out of only one side of the brain lives an incomplete existence. The same can be said of personal- ity development; if we function with only one side of our being, we have limited opportunity for change. To become aware of the visual, intuitive, image-making functions is not to let go of the verbal, rational functions, but to learn to operate more fully through both. The more we learn to use the wide variety of ingredients that make up the structure of personality, the more whole we will become.

We are all dominated by the conscious side of personality. The task of meeting the face of our unconscious is not easy. Because the therapist has the well-trained eye of an outside observer, he or she is an excellent tool for psychological growth. Many dimensions of the psyche that are encountered by the inner artist are not acceptable to the ego. Figures of our negative aspects, revealed through such images as *Disease, Devourer, The Witch Woman, Wild Beasts, The Inner Critic* and *The Evaluator*, are not brought into consciousness graciously. If we work to achieve an inclusive wholeness, the time, money and energy invested in therapy will prove invaluable.

As therapists and clients work together at the process of self-discovery, it's important to keep in mind these comments from Jung:

We must be able to let things happen in the psyche. For us, this actually is an art of which few people know anything. Consciousness is forever interfering, helping, correcting, and negating, and never leaving the simple growth of the psychic processes in peace.... To begin with, the task consists solely in objectively observing a fragment of a fantasy in its development. Nothing could be simpler, and yet right here the difficulties begin.... The conscious mind ... often seems bent upon blotting out the spontaneous fantasy-activity in spite of real insight, even of firm determination on the part of the individual to allow the psychic processes to go forward without interference. Often a veritable cramp of consciousness exists.[38]

The therapist's task is to help relieve such a "cramp in consciousness" through the support and encouragement of as much of the client's personality as can be glimpsed. An image, a poem or a dream that might otherwise be dismissed is honored and nurtured when taken to the therapy hour. Moving beyond the limits of talk therapy to include images introduces a verbal-visual perspective that enhances the therapeutic impact.

If we want to work in therapy with our images, we must be brave enough to look for, and look at, the truth. If we choose not to work with a psyche/soul therapist, then we place upon ourselves the enormous burden of being completely honest with ourselves. A therapist will often ask the question that brings out the psychological truth we have been avoiding. The inner artist will ask the same soul-searching questions and we must be willing to stay with what she presents. The ongoing development of our full being is not an easy path to follow, but surely it is no more difficult than the various ways in which we keep ourselves unconscious and unchanging.

Not to grow and change is unnatural. If we refuse our opportunities for wholeness through connection to the Center, we short-circuit our own humanity. On the other hand, if we dare to risk the full blossoming of our souls, we reap the fruits of a dynamic and multifaceted life.

Appendix: Suggested Materials

The items marked with an asterisk are the basic necessities to enable you to do the exercises in this book. Begin with a few and add to your collection as your interest grows.

A white drawing tablet of a comfortable size*
Colored construction paper
Felt tip pens—fine points, mixed colors
Soft-lead pencils*
Art gum eraser*
Crayons
Chalk
Oil pastels*
Box of water colors
Brushes of various sizes
Acrylic paint in small tubes
Scissors, glue
A small block of clay
A box in which you save odds and ends such
    as colored yarn, ribbon, leaves, shells,
    flowers, feathers, old photographs, pic-
    tures from magazines, etc.
A journal or artist's sketch book. I prefer a
    bound sketch book in standard 8×11 size
    so that I can write on one side and create
    images on the other.*

Notes

1. Betty Edwards, *Drawing On the Artist Within* (New York: Simon & Schuster, 1986), p. 50.
2. Ibid., p. 103.
3. R.J. Lifton and R. Falk, *Indefensible Weapons* (New York: Basic Books, 1982), p. 39.
4. M.L. von Franz, "The Process of Individuation", in *Man and His Symbols*, ed. Carl Jung and M.L. von Franz (New York: Doubleday, 1964), p. 174.
5. Nancy Wood, *Many Winters* (New York: Doubleday, 1974), p. 50.
6. Jean Shinoda Bolen, *Goddesses in Everywoman* (New York: Harper & Row, 1985), p. 43 passim.
7. Robert A. Johnson, *Inner Work* (San Francisco: Harper & Row, 1986), p. 138.
8. *The New Jerusalem Bible* (New York: Doubleday, 1970), Genesis 3:1.
9. Rainer Maria Rilke, *Letters to a Young Poet*, trans. Stephen Mitchell (New York: Random House, 1984), p. 92.
10. Carl G. Jung, *Mandala Symbolism* (Princeton, N.J.: Princeton University Press, 1969), p. 5.
11. Aniela Jaffe, *The Myth of Meaning* (New York: Putnam, 1971), p. 37.
12. Shunryu Suzuki, *Zen Mind, Beginner's Mind* (New York and Tokyo: Weatherhill, 1970), p. 25.
13. Edward F. Edinger, *Ego and Archetype* (New York: Penguin, 1972), p. 37.

14. Charles Williams, *The Greater Trumps* (London: William B. Eerdmans, 1950), p. 30 passim.

15. James Hillman, *Insearch: Psychology and Religion* (Dallas: Spring, 1979), p. 22.

16. Mary C. Fullerson, *The Form of the Fourth* (Berkeley: Shambhala, 1971), p. 79.

17. Carlos Castaneda, *The Fire From Within* (New York: Simon & Schuster, 1984), p. 84.

18. Ken Wilber, *No Boundary* (Boulder: Shambhala, 1979), p. 45.

19. Frederick Franck, *The Awakened Eye* (New York: Random House, 1979), pp. 56-9.

20. Thomas Peters and Robert Waterman, *In Search of Excellence* (New York: Warner, 1982), p. 60.

21. This exercise is by Alice Lloyd Heaton Allen.

22. Betty Edwards, *Drawing on the Right Side of the Brain* (Los Angeles: J.P. Tarcher, 1979), p. 52.

23. Sallie Nichols, *Jung and Tarot: An Archetypal Journey* (York Beach, Maine: Samuel Weiser, 1980), p. 30.

24. Paul Radin, *The Trickster* (New York: Schocken, 1978), p. 184.

25. Nichols, *Jung and Tarot*, p. 24.

26. Milton Klonsky, *Blake's Dante* (New York: Crown, 1980), p. 6.

27. Viktor E. Frankl, *The Unheard Cry for Meaning* (New York: Simon & Schuster, 1978), p. 35.

28. James Hillman, *Re-Visioning Psychology* (New York: Harper & Row, 1975), p. 23.

29. Allen, Alice Lloyd Heaton, "Discovering My Personal Myth Through Spontaneous Art Media" (Master's thesis, Sonoma State College, CA, 1971), p. 35.

30. Suzuki, *Zen Mind, Beginner's Mind*, p. 78.

31. Werner Haftmann, *Chagall*, trans. Heinrich Baumann and Alexis Brown (New York: Abrams, 1984), p. 52.

32. Suzuki, *Zen Mind, Beginner's Mind*, p. 80.

33. Lao Tsu, *Tao Te Ching*, trans. Gia-fu Feng and Jane English (New York: Random House, 1975), p. 1.

34. James Douglass, *Lightning East to West* (New York: Crossroad, 1983), p. 37.

35. Rilke, *Letters to a Young Poet*, p. 20.

36. Carl G. Jung, *Memories, Dreams, Reflections* (New York: Random House, 1961), p. 401.

37. Carl G. Jung, *The Portable Jung*, ed. Joseph Campbell (New York: Penguin, 1971), p. 289.

38. Richard Wilhelm and C.G. Jung, *The Secret of the Golden Flower* (New York: Harcourt Brace Jovanovich, 1931), p. 93.

Bibliography

Allen, Alice Lloyd Heaton. "Discovering My Personal Myth Through Spontaneous Art Media." Master's Thesis. Sonoma State College, Rohnert Park, California, 1971.

Bolen, Jean Shinoda. *Goddesses in Everywoman.* New York: Harper & Row, 1985.

Castaneda, Carlos. *The Fire From Within.* New York: Simon & Schuster, 1984.

Douglass, James. *Lightning East to West.* New York: Crossroad, 1983.

Edinger, Edward F. *Ego and Archetype.* New York: Penguin, 1972.

Edwards, Betty. *Drawing on the Artist Within.* New York: Simon & Schuster, 1986.

———. *Drawing on the Right Side of the Brain.* Los Angeles: J.P. Tarcher, 1979.

Franck, Frederick. *The Awakened Eye.* New York: Random House, 1979.

Frankl, Viktor E. *The Unheard Cry for Meaning.* New York: Simon & Schuster, 1978.

Fullerson, Mary C. *The Form of the Fourth.* Berkeley: Shambhala, 1971.

Haftmann, Werner. *Chagall.* Translated by Heinrich Baumann and Alexis Brown. New York: Harry N. Abrams, Inc., 1984.

Hillman, James. *Insearch: Psychology and Religion.* Dallas: Spring, 1979.

———. *Re-Visioning Psychology.* New York: Harper & Row, 1975.

Jaffe, Aniela. *The Myth of Meaning.* New York: Putnam, 1971.

Johnson, Robert A. *Inner Work.* San Francisco: Harper & Row, 1986.

Jung, Carl G. and von Franz, M.L., eds. *Man and His Symbols.* New York: Doubleday, 1964.

Jung, Carl G. *Mandala Symbolism.* Princeton, N.J.: Princeton University Press, 1969.

———. *Memories, Dreams, Reflections.* New York: Random House, 1961.

———. *The Portable Jung.* New York: Viking, 1971.

Klonsky, Milton. *Blake's Dante.* New York: Crown, 1980.

Lao Tsu. *Tao Te Ching.* Translated by Gia-fu Feng and Jane English. New York: Random House, 1975.

Lifton, R.J. and Falk, R. *Indefensible Weapons.* New York: Basic Books, 1982.

The New Jerusalem Bible. New York: Doubleday, 1970.

Nichols, Sallie. *Jung and Tarot: An Archetypal Journey.* York Beach, Maine: Samuel Weiser, 1980.

Peters, Thomas and Waterman, Robert. *In Search of Excellence.* New York: Warner, 1982.

Radin, Paul. *The Trickster.* New York: Schocken, 1978.

Rilke, Rainer Maria. *Letters to a Young Poet.* Translated by Stephen Mitchell. New York: Random House, 1984.

Suzuki, Shunryu. *Zen Mind, Beginner's Mind.* New York and Tokyo: Weatherhill, 1970.

Wilber, Ken. *No Boundary.* Boulder: Shambhala, 1979.

Wilhelm, Richard and Jung, Carl G. *The Secret of the Golden Flower*. New York: Harcourt Brace Jovanovich, 1931.

Williams, Charles. *The Greater Trumps*. London: William B. Eerdmans, 1950.

Wood, Nancy. *Many Winters*. New York: Doubleday, 1974.